Highly regarded as a well-organized, concise, and balanced summary of the present status of scholarship on the issues, this first English translation of a distinguished German work will be of special interest to biblical scholars, Old Testament specialists, students, and professors.

JOACHIM BECKER is Professor of Old Testament at the Collegium Damianeum at Simpelveld, the Netherlands.

Messianic Expectation in the Old Testament

Messianic Expectation in the Old Testament

by
JOACHIM BECKER

translated by
DAVID E. GREEN

FORTRESS PRESS   Philadelphia

This book is a translation of *Messiaserwartung im Alten Testament,* copyright © 1977 by Verlag Katholisches Bibelwerk GmbH in Stuttgart, Germany.

Biblical quotations from the Revised Standard Version of the Bible, copyright 1946, 1952, © 1971, 1973 by the Division of Christian Education of the National Council of the Churches of Christ in the U.S.A., are used by permission.

Library of Congress Cataloging in Publication Data

Becker, Joachim, 1931-
   Messianic expectation in the Old Testament.

   Translation of Messiaserwartung im Alten Testament.
   Includes bibliographical references.
   1. Messiah—Biblical teaching. 2. Bible. O.T.—
Criticism, interpretation, etc. I. Title.
BS680.M4B413   296.3'3   79-8891
ISBN 0–8006–0545–4

8023K79   Printed in the United States of America   1-545

Contents

Abbreviations

AASF	Annales academiae scientiarum Fennicae
AGSU	Arbeiten zur Geschichte des Spätjudentums und Urchristentums
AnBib	Analecta biblica
Ang.	Angelicum
AOAT	Alter Orient und Altes Testament
AThD	Acta theologica Danica
AzT	Arbeiten zur Theologie
BBB	Bonner biblische Beiträge
BEThL	Bibliotheca ephemeridum theologicarum Lovaniensium
BFCTL	Bibliothèque de la faculté catholique de théologie de Lyon
BHTh	Beiträge zur historischen Theologie
Bib.	Biblica
Bijd.	Bijdragen
BiLi	Bibel und Liturgie
BK	Biblischer Kommentar
BSt	Biblische Studien, Neukirchen
BWANT	Beiträge zur Wissenschaft vom Alten und Neuen Testament
BZ	Biblische Zeitschrift
BZAW	Beihefte zur Zeitschrift für die Alttestamentliche Wissenschaft
BZNW	Beihefte zur Zeitschrift für die Neutestamentliche Wissenschaft

BZSF	Biblische Zeit- und Streitfragen zur Aufklärung der Gebildeten
CBQ	*Catholic Biblical Quarterly*
CRB	Cahiers de la Revue biblique
EHS.T	Europäische Hochschulschriften: Reihe 23, Theologie
ESt	Eichstätter Studien
EstB	*Estudios bíblicos*
ÉtB	Études bibliques
EThL	*Ephemerides theologicae Lovanienses*
EvTh	*Evangelische Theologie*
FDV	Franz-Delitzsch-Vorlesungen
FRLANT	Forschungen zur Religion und Literatur des Alten und Neuen Testaments
FThSt	Freiburger theologische Studien
FTS	Frankfurter theologische Studien
FzB	Forschung zur Bibel
HAT	Handbuch zum Alten Testament
HK	Handkommentar zum Alten Testament
HUCA	*Hebrew Union College Annual*
JBL	*Journal of Biblical Literature*
JQR	*Jewish Quarterly Review*
JSJ	*Journal for the Study of Judaism*
Jud.	*Judaica*
KAT	Kommentar zum Alten Testament
KuD	*Kerygma und Dogma*
LeDiv	Lectio divina
LTP	*Laval théologique et philosophique*
MHUC	Monographs of the Hebrew Union College
NRTh	*Nouvelle revue théologique*
OBO	Orbis biblicus et orientalis
OTL	Old Testament Library
PTh	Pastoraltheologie
RB	*Revue biblique*
RdQ	*Revue de Qumran*
RechBib	Recherches bibliques
RevSR	*Revue des sciences religieuses*
RThom	*Revue thomiste*

RThPh	*Revue de théologie et de philosophie*
RWB	Religionswissenschaftliche Bibliothek
SBM	Stuttgarter biblische Monographien
SBS	Stuttgarter Bibelstudien
Sem.	*Semitica*
SJ	Studia Judaica
SJI	Studien aus dem C. G. Jung-Institut
SKG.G	Schriften der Königsberger Gelehrten Gesellschaft. Geisteswissenschaftliche Reihe
SSN	Studia semitica Neerlandica
StANT	Studien zum Alten und Neuen Testament
StNT	Studien zum Neuen Testament
StT	Studi e testi
StTh	*Studia theologica, Lund*
StUNT	Studien zur Umwelt des Neuen Testaments
TB	Theologische Bücherei
ThGl	Theologie und Glaube
ThLZ	*Theologische Literaturzeitung*
ThPh	*Theologie und Philosophie*
ThRv	*Theologische Revue*
ThViat	*Theologia viatorum*
ThZ	*Theologische Zeitschrift*
TICP	Travaux de l'institut catholique de Paris
TThQ	*Tübinger theologische Quartalschrift*
TTL	Theological Translation Library
VD	*Verbum domini*
VT	*Vetus Testamentum*
VT.S	Supplements to Vetus Testamentum
WMANT	Wissenschaftliche Monographien zum Alten und Neuen Testament
WSAMA.T	Walberger Studien der Albertus-Magnus-Akademie. Theologische Reihe
WZ(L).GS	*Wissenschaftliche Zeitschrift der Karl-Marx-Universität Leipzig. Gesellschafts- und sprachwissenschaftliche Reihe*
ZAW	*Zeitschrift für die Alttestamentliche Wissenschaft*
ZBK	Zürcher Bibelkommentar

ZDMG.S	Zeitschrift der deutschen Morgenlaendischen Gesellschaft. Supplementa
ZKTh	*Zeitschrift für katholische Theologie*
ZThK	*Zeitschrift für Theologie und Kirche*

1

The Perspective of the
New Testament and the Church

The New Testament, the tradition of the church, and traditional apologetics all assume that in the Old Testament the messiah is awaited and his coming is proclaimed in advance. Our purpose in the present study is not to sketch this post–Old Testament picture of messianic expectation, but we must begin with at least an outline of it. It calls for historical-critical inquiry into its roots and provides a foil against which to measure the results of our historical quest. Above all, it is an inalienable component of the faith proclaimed by the church. We must return to it in our conclusion.

The New Testament, the tradition of the church, and traditional apologetics do not in fact share a wholly common perspective. The New Testament cites a wealth of messianic passages ignored by scholarly apologetics as instances of purely external accommodation. On the other hand, some passages (such as Gen. 3:15) play a role in the ecclesiastical and apologetic image of the messianic expectation although—perhaps by chance—they are scarcely mentioned in the New Testament. There is nevertheless some justification for reducing the New Testament, the tradition of the church, and apologetics to a common denominator. In any case, they agree in thinking in terms of an unbroken stream of messianic expectation and clear prediction.

It will suffice for our purposes to follow the approach of traditional apologetics, which considers itself a critical selection of New Testament passages. The first prediction of the redeemer

11

appears in Gen. 3:15. The line of the promise runs through Seth, Noah, and Shem to Abraham, who marks a crossroads in sacral history. Always—as suggested in Romans 4 and Gal. 3:16ff.—the *person* of the redeemer is included in the promise. Passing through Isaac and Jacob, the line of the promise narrows continually down to Jacob's son Judah. In Gen. 49:8–12, the next standard passage after Gen. 3:15, we learn that the messiah will spring from the tribe of Judah. The reader who thinks in historical terms must be surprised that there is no other mention of the person of the redeemer in the patriarchal period. Neither is there any mention in the ancient period of the Exodus, Sinai, and the desert. Only the fourth Balaam oracle (Num. 24:15–24) knows anything of a king arising in Jacob. The accounts of the occupation of Canaan and the period of the Judges likewise require that we postulate a subterranean stream of messianic expectation.

With the prophecy of Nathan (2 Samuel 7) a new landmark is set up: the messiah will be a descendant of David within the tribe of Judah. From now on, expectation of the messiah is linked with the fate of the house of David. Explicit evidence, to be sure, does not appear until two centuries later in Isaiah (7:14; 8:23— 9:6 [Eng. 9:1–7]; 11:1–10), Micah (5:1–5[2–6]), Amos (9:11), and Hosea (3:5). A kind of substitute for the missing evidence appears in the messianic psalms (2, 45, 72, 89, 110, 132), which are all considered preexilic. At the end of the monarchy and the beginning of the Exile, passages in Jeremiah and Ezekiel furnish the welcome proof that we are dealing with a continuously flowing stream of expectation, surfacing occasionally, which hastens onward to its goal of fulfillment.

The stream metaphor is complemented by the notion of an increasingly clear mosaic image. In the exilic period, to which modern critical apologetics is happy to assign Deutero-Isaiah (Isaiah 40–55), the songs of the servant of Yahweh present a deepened and spiritualized picture of the messiah. The early postexilic evidence of Zech. 9:9–10 and 12:10 (possibly with Zechariah 3, 4, and 6, as well as Hag. 2:20–23) is followed by an alarming barren period. The passage concerning the son of man in Daniel 7 and the prophecy of seventy weeks in Dan. 9:24–27 are once again striking messianic prophecies. The latter text probably even led to ill-conceived attempts to calculate the date of the messiah's coming.

There has been no lack of attempts to replace this highly vulnerable picture of messianic expectation with a critically responsible outline.[1] Nevertheless, even the most critical scholars still seem to stand under the influence of the traditional perspective when weighing the purely historical facts, and there is justification for a new attempt to investigate the historical data.[2]

---

1. Cf. especially Sigmund Mowinckel, *He That Cometh*, trans. G. W. Anderson (Oxford: Blackwell, 1956); Martin Rehm, *Der königliche Messias im Licht der Immanuel-Weissagungen des Buches Jesaja* ESt, n.f., Bd. 1 (Kevelaer: Butzon und Bercker, 1968) (cf. my review in *ThRv* 77 [1971]: 21–24); Joseph Coppens, *Le messianisme royal*, LeDiv 54 (Paris: Editions du Cerf, 1968), reprinted from *NRTh* 90 (1968): 30–49, 225–51, 479–512, 622–50, 834–63, 936–75; Ulrich Kellermann, *Messias und Gesetz*, BSt 61 (Neukirchen: Neukirchener Verlag, 1971). For an introduction to later developments in Judaism, a useful outline is Ferdinand Dexinger, "Die Entwicklung des jüdisch-christlichen Messianismus," *BiLi* 47 (1974): 5–31, 239–66.

2. Cf. already Joachim Becker, *Isaias: Der Prophet und sein Buch*, SBS 30 (Stuttgart: Katholisches Bibelwerk, 1968); idem, "Das historische Bild der messianischen Erwartung im Alten Testament," in *Testimonium veritati*, ed. Hans Wolter, FTS 7 (Frankfurt: Knecht, 1971), pp. 125–41.

2

Antimonarchic Movements in Israel

It is only to be expected that the nation of the messiah would have a special relationship to kingship from the very beginning, since kingship is the foundation of the messianic expectation. Historical observation must, however, recognize the paradox that kingship appeared suspect to early Yahwism.[1] It is a simple fact that at one time Israel lived without a king. May there even have been a sense of theocracy that made human ("empirical") kingship impossible because only Yahweh could be king in Israel? This question is raised primarily by the words of Gideon in Judg. 8:22–23 and by certain passages in the narrative context of 1 Samuel 8–15. Here earthly kingship is rejected or questioned with reference to the kingship of Yahweh.[2] The crucial question

---

1. See Jean de Fraine, *L'aspect religieux de la royauté israélite*, AnBib 3 (Rome: Pontificio Istituto Biblico, 1954); Martin Buber, *Kingship of God*, trans. R. Scheimann (New York: Harper, 1967); Eugene H. Maly, "Affectus anti-monarchicus in Israel praeexilico," *VD* 37 (1959): 353–56 (summary of a dissertation); idem, "The Jotham Fable—Antimonarchical?" *CBQ* 22 (1960): 299–305; Karl Heinz Bernhardt, *Das Problem der altorientalischen Königsideologie im Alten Testament*, VT.S 8 (Leiden: Brill, 1961), pp. 91–182; J. Alberto Soggin, *Das Königtum in Israel*, BZAW 104 (Berlin: Töpelmann, 1967); Hans Jochen Boecker, *Die Beurteilung der Anfänge des Königtums in den deuteronomistischen Abschnitten des 1. Samuelbuches*, WMANT 31 (Neukirchen: Neukirchener Verlag, 1969); F. Langlamet, "Les récits de l'institution de la royauté (I Sam. VII–XII)," *RB* 77 (1970): 161–200; Werner H. Schmidt, "Kritik am Königtum," in *Probleme biblischer Theologie* (Festschrift G. von Rad), ed. H. W. Wolff (Munich: Kaiser, 1971), pp. 440–61.

2. In 1 Samuel 8–15, the antimonarchic position appears only in one particular literary stratum, which probably also includes 8:1–22; 10:17–27;

14

is: Do such passages faithfully express the historical consciousness of the period of the Judges, or do they merely reflect the consciousness of a later period, which had had negative experiences with kingship? The answer depends on more than just the date of the texts; a later writer can record the consciousness of an earlier age. And of course no scholar claims that the account was written by a contemporary of the events.[3] The decision therefore lies in the murky realm of tradition criticism, where, as we would expect, opinions differ.

The theocratic statements of Gideon and Samuel are usually taken to be retrojections of a later conviction. If so, we are in the intellectual milieu of the Deuteronomistic age, dating at the earliest toward the end of the monarchy. References to the kingship as belonging to Yahweh alone are anachronistic, if only because this idea was borrowed from the Canaanite world and was therefore not a factor in earliest Israel.[4] This is the majority opinion, but there are those who find in the accounts an authentic witness to an early Israelite conviction.[5]

---

and 12:1–25 (see especially 8:5–22; 10:19; 12:12–14, 17, 19). Detailed analysis of the two or three literary strata is not necessary for our purpose. The reader may consult the works of Soggin, Boecker, and Langlamet cited in note 1, above. The promonarchic stratum comprises 9:1–10, 16; 13:5–15. The view that the narrative is homogeneous (Martin Buber, "Die Erzählung von Sauls Königswahl," *VT* 6 [1956]: 113–73) does not merit support.

3. Scholars differ as to the exact dating of these passages (which is not critical for our investigation). According to Wolfgang Richter, *Traditionsgeschichtliche Untersuchungen zum Richterbuch*, BBB 18, 2d ed. (Bonn: Hanstein, 1966), the words of Gideon come from an antimonarchic "book of deliverers" composed in the ninth century B.C. The Elohistic source of the Heptateuch and a Deuteronomistic writer have also been suggested. Walter Beyerlin, "Geschichte und heilsgeschichtliche Traditionsbildung im Alten Testament," *VT* 13 (1963): 1–25, thinks in terms of a stratum concerned with Israel as a whole, which must therefore be late. The antimonarchic passages in 1 Samuel 8–15 are often ascribed to a Deuteronomistic writer.

4. See, for example, Albrecht Alt, "Gedanken über das Königtum Jahwes," in his *Kleine Schriften* (Munich: Beck, 1953–59), 1:345–57; Werner Schmidt, *Königtum Gottes in Ugarit und Israel*, BZAW 80, 2d ed. (Berlin: Töpelmann, 1966).

5. See, for example, Artur Weiser, *Samuel: Seine geschichtliche Aufgabe und religiöse Bedeutung*, FRLANT 81 (Göttingen: Vandenhoeck, 1962). Of primary importance is the balanced discussion in Soggin, *Königtum*, pp. 15–20, 31–38. This position is developed most fully by Buber, *Kingship*. He elaborates an antithesis between the early Israelite *"malk"* kingship of

We will seek a mediating position. The hypothesis of a retrospective theological interpretation of history is justified. What is often overlooked is that this interpretation does not reject kingship per se but wishes rather to relativize kingship within the context of Yahwism.[6] The dialogues and remonstrances in 1 Samuel 8, 10, and 12, which are probably Deuteronomistic, suggest the sham controversies of a worried theologian who is fundamentally in favor of a monarchy with Yahwistic constraints. We must then go on to ask, however, whether this cautious evaluation of the monarchy has not incorporated an element of the early Israelite conviction on the question. Retrojection may be assumed, but it is not total. There was probably an antimonarchic conviction in ancient Israel that did not depend on a theological reference to the kingship of Yahweh but had sociological roots. The Israelites were originally seminomads having a social structure dominated by associations of tribes and clans; for a long period they were alien to the settled territory and its institutions, including kingship. This accounts for the appearance of someone like Ahijah of Shiloh, with his attack on Solomon, the opposition of the prophets during the ninth century B.C., and the antimonarchic statements of Hosea, which are motivated by more than religious considerations. During the period of the monarchy, we must reckon with a difference in mentality between the tradition-bound Israelites of the countryside and the royal cities, more influenced by the Canaanites. In Judg. 8:22–23 and 1 Samuel 8, 10, 12, the interpreters of history turned a sociological position into a theological position.

Yahweh (God as leader of the people) and the Baal kingship of the earth-bound fertility deities of Canaan. He calls the Jotham fable "the strongest anti-monarchial poem of world literature" (p. 75; for a contrary view, see Maly, "Jotham Fable"). In the Book of Judges, he distinguishes the antimonarchic chapters 1–12, in which the words of Gideon and the fable of Jotham appear, from the promonarchic chapters 17–21 (see 17:6; 18:1; 19:1; 21:25).

6. This point is made by Weiser (*Samuel*), for whom, however, the historical interpretation fits the historical conviction of the time of Solomon, and above all by Boecker (*Beurteilung*). For a discussion of the positive evaluation of the kingship on the part of the Deuteronomist, see below, Chapter 8.

Hostility to the monarchy is therefore just one element in a general attitude of reserve toward the institutions of the civilized territory. These include the introduction of Baal worship into the cult, the mercenary army, the public life of the cities, and the organization of the state.[7] This background accounts for the opposition to the census in 2 Samuel 24. Even the building of the temple must have appeared suspect to orthodox Yahwism. Only Solomon was capable of an enterprise so contrary to tradition; a long time passed before it was recognized as genuinely Israelite. How tenaciously the ancient Israelite sense of life endured can be observed in the curious sociological phenomenon of the Rechabites, who even at the end of the period of the monarchy rejected the way of life of the civilized territory; characteristically, they were ardent worshipers of Yahweh.[8]

The reflections of this chapter strike at the root of the illusory hypothesis of an early messianic expectation that continued throughout the Old Testament period. The prerequisites were not even present. The concept of kingship, an important category for sacral history, was not integrated until late in Israel's history, and then only in a reduced format acceptable to Yahwism.[9] In sacral history it is not unexampled for important categories to come into play later from outside. Instances include the various notions of a life to come, belief in angels and demons, and the idea of redemption, which were at least enriched by Parseeism and gnosticlike movements.

---

7. See the material assembled under the heading "Nomadism and Its Survival" in Roland de Vaux, *Ancient Israel*, trans. J. McHugh (New York: McGraw-Hill, 1961), pp. 3–15.

8. See 2 Kings 10:15–16, 23; Jeremiah 35.

9. This refers to the purified notion of the king typical of restorative monarchism (see below, Chapters 8 and 9).

3

The Davidic Monopoly

When the monarchy was looked on with favor in Israel, it was not limited from the start to the Davidic monarchy, through which, in the view of late Judaism and the New Testament, runs the line of salvation. Without calling into question the value of this view with respect to sacral history, we shall search out the historical convictions of the early period. The later view can already be discerned in the historical presentation of the Old Testament itself. The Deuteronomistic History, which was completed during the Exile, undertakes certain shifts that distort the view of historical reality. It defends the sole legitimacy of the Davidic monarchy, while characterizing the monarchy of the Northern Kingdom as an illegitimate offshoot without any future. David is presented accordingly as the first Israelite king.

Let us begin with this latter point, which only appears to be incidental. Saul is introduced as a preliminary countertype, helping to depict the rise of David. This picture may correspond more or less to historical reality. At the same time, we find here a bias of the Deuteronomistic History, and the lines are retraced with vigor. The historian intervenes radically when figures from the period of the Judges might have some claim to having been if not king *of* Israel at least king *in* Israel. There simply must be no king before David (and Saul). The Book of Judges makes Gideon a "judge," although there is evidence that he was a king. According to Judg. 8:30, he had a harem and seventy sons, which suggests dynastic aspirations. Although Judg. 8:22–23 indicates that he refused the kingship for theocratic reasons, in 8:27 he

18

requests the jewelry taken in battle in order to make an ephod (probably a cultic image). In his own city of Ophrah in the tribe of Manasseh he established a sanctuary; in the view of the ancient Near East, this can be considered an essential element of kingship.[1] Even the biblical account admits that Abimelech, one of Gideon's sons, was king in Shechem (Judges 9), although not without elaborating a reprehensible episode. Jephthah (Judg. 11:1—12:7), like David, was a leader of mercenaries and an insurgent. According to Judg. 10:18 and 11:6, 7, 11, he was leader ($q\bar{a}ṣîn$) and head ($r\bar{o}'š$)[2] of his tribal associates. Judges 11:11 suggests an enthronement ceremony at the sanctuary in Mizpah, based on a compact ("words"). This is probably also the form in which David received the kingship over Judah and Israel. In its outward manifestations, the kingship of Saul probably did not differ greatly from the role of Gideon, Abimelech, and Jephthah. Scholarship generally emphasizes that it was a charismatic and democratic kingship involving leadership of the militia, in contrast to the kingship of David and Solomon.[3] If necessary, Saul could have been made into a judge. The Old Testament account probably based its orientation on Saul's kingship having been the first to claim authority over all Israel and its close association with the rise of David.

It is possible that during the period of the Judges there were institutions similar to kingship with extended authority. The his-

---

1. Gideon's kingship is denied by Eugen Täubler, *Biblische Studien*, ed. H. J. Zobel (Tübingen: Mohr, 1958), pp. 267ff. According to Gwynne Henton Davies, "Judges VIII, 22–23," *VT* 13 (1963): 151–57, in Judg. 8:22–23 Gideon not only did not refuse the kingship but accepted it positively. Whatever the truth may be, this interpretation ignores the narrative purpose of the Deuteronomistic History. On the question of whether Gideon and Jerubbaal are two distinct historical figures, see Herbert Haag, "Gideon —Jerubbaal—Abimelek," *ZAW* 79 (1967): 305–14.

2. See John R. Bartlett, "The Use of the Word *rō'š* as a Title in the Old Testament," *VT* 19 (1969): 1–10.

3. Contrariwise, the institutional features of Saul's kingship are emphasized by Walter Beyerlin, "Das Königscharisma bei Saul," *ZAW* 73 (1961): 186–201. Ludwig Schmidt, *Menschlicher Erfolg und Jahwes Initiative*, WMANT 38 (Neukirchen: Neukirchener Verlag, 1970), likewise sees a difference from charismatic militia kingship, pointing to the institution of a mercenary army (cf. 1 Sam. 10:26; 13:2; 14:2, 52).

torical function of the judges is far from clear. A true institution may lie behind the "minor" judges, named only in lists. Within the framework of his amphictyonic theory, Noth[4] views them as expounders of the sacral law governing the tribes. Richter[5] considers the office of judge an organ of civil government and the administration of justice, as demanded by life in the civilized territory. This would imply a kind of preliminary stage leading toward the monarchy. Soggin,[6] too, argues for an organic development and points out analogous phenomena among the seminomads and nomads.

In addition, we must consider the term $n\bar{a}g\hat{i}d$,[7] which is still applied in formulaic expressions to David, Solomon, and the kings of the Northern Kingdom. We may be dealing with a mere synonym of *melek*, "king," which refers to the king to the extent that he has been designated by Yahweh. Its etymology can be associated with the concept of designation; the more general meaning "leader, prince," could represent semantic extension. Richter and Schmidt, however, hypothesize that there was a $n\bar{a}g\bar{i}d$ institution in the period of the Judges, namely, the charismatic military leader in the holy war; according to Richter, he was expressly designated by prophets.

But now to the central question of the Davidic monopoly on legitimacy. The later privilege undoubtedly rests on a strong foundation in fact. David was a man of achievement and the founder of an empire. After a preliminary phase as a vassal king of the Philistines in Ziklag, he ruled over Judah (2 Sam. 2:4) and

---

4. Martin Noth, "Das Amt des 'Richters Israels,'" in *Festschrift Alfred Bertholet*, ed. W. Baumgartner et al. (Tübingen: Mohr, 1950), pp. 404–17, reprinted in his *Gesammelte Studien zum Alten Testament*, ed. H. W. Wolff, TB 6, 39 (Munich: Kaiser, 1966–69), 2:71–85.

5. Wolfgang Richter, "Zu den 'Richtern Israels,'" *ZAW* 77 (1965): 40–72.

6. *Königtum*, pp. 11–25, 149–62.

7. See Wolfgang Richter, "Die nāgīd-Formel," *BZ*, n.f. 9 (1965): 71–84; idem, *Die sogenannten vorprophetischen Berufungsberichte*, FRLANT 101 (Göttingen: Vandenhoeck, 1970); Schmidt, *Menschlicher Erfolg*, pp. 141–71; Langlamet, "Récits," pp. 188–99; E. Lipiński, "Nāgīd, der Kronprinz," *VT* 24 (1974): 497–99.

the northern tribes (2 Sam. 5:3) as two separate entities, much after the manner of Saul's kingship. At Jerusalem he ruled in Canaanite style. In addition, he held the kingship of the Ammonites (2 Sam. 12:30) and maintained a system of vassal kings.[8] David respected Israelite sensibilities, which saved him from the fate of Saul and the ill-advised incaution of Solomon.[9] The halo surrounding the Davidic monarchy was made even brighter by the fact that the fragile conglomeration of David's empire was able to endure for a period under Solomon and by the uninterrupted reign of the Davidic dynasty until the end of the Judahite state. Whether Solomon's successors could have maintained his absolutism is dubious. The tribal territory of Judah was always different from the royal residence of Jerusalem.[10] Nevertheless, the rural aristocracy of Judah (*'am hā'āreṣ*) always remained faithful to the royal house of David.[11] Most of all, the Davidic dynasty profited from the early fall of the Northern Kingdom and national disintegration of the northern tribes.

It does not follow, however, that the Davidic dynasty occupied a special place in sacral history in the eyes of the preexilic period. The question probably did not even arise. Historical analysis reveals a political superiority of the Northern Kingdom, to which Judah was subject for a period as a vassal state. The Northern Kingdom incorporated the majority of the tribes. It was as a whole more bound to tradition and more authentically Israelite. The ancient traditions (exodus from Egypt, Sinai, occupation of

---

8. On the nature of the Davidic monarchy, see Albrecht Alt, "The Formation of the Israelite State in Palestine," in his *Essays on Old Testament History and Religion*, trans. R. A. Wilson (Oxford: Blackwell, 1966), pp. 1–65; idem, "Das Grossreich Davids," *ThLZ* 75 (1950): 213–20, reprinted in his *Kleine Schriften zur Geschichte des Volkes Israel*, 3 vols. (Munich: Beck, 1953–59), 2:66–75; idem, "The Monarchy in Israel and Judah," in his *Essays*, pp. 239–60; Martin Noth, "Gott, König, Volk im Alten Testament," *ZThK* 47 (1950): 157–91, reprinted in his *Gesammelte Studien*, 1:188–229; Schmidt, *Menschlicher Erfolg;* Soggin, *Königtum*, pp. 58–76.
9. Solomon's innovations (temple, chariotry, strict administration, elimination of the Shiloh priesthood) are treated with indulgence and even glorified by the Old Testament. Only his religious syncretism is stigmatized.
10. Note Isaiah's phrase "Jerusalem and Judah" in Isa. 3:1, 8; 5:3; 22:21.
11. See 2 Kings 11:14, 20; 14:21; 21:24; 23:30.

Canaan) appear to have their locus in the north.[12] The circumstance that the sanctuaries of Bethel and Dan (schismatic in the eyes of the Deuteronomist) had more tradition behind them than Jerusalem probably influenced contemporaries. Amos, whose homeland was Judah, exercised his ministry in Bethel (and Samaria). None of his authentic oracles mentions Jerusalem. Possibly it seemed to him, a religious conservative, not sufficiently Israelite. It is not necessary to ask whether a prophet like Elijah felt any bond with Jerusalem. It is not by chance that the name "Israel" continued to be the political term for the Northern Kingdom. The division of the empire after the death of Solomon, in light of the continuing dualism of north and south, was a normal process, involving nothing more than dissolution of a personal union. Even the pro-Judah account of 1 Kings 11:29–39 does not deny that the prophet Ahijah of Shiloh supported the division; he does not even conceal the promise of eternal endurance to the house of Jeroboam I (see vv. 38–39).

The "sin of Jeroboam" constantly spoken of by the Deuteronomist proves to be an anachronism.[13] The charges refer to Jeroboam's offense against the unity of the cult through his establishment of sanctuaries at Bethel and Dan, his construction of bull images in these sanctuaries, his toleration of the local high places, his appointment of priests who were not Levites, and his changing the date of the autumn festival (see especially 1 Kings

---

12. The geographical separation between the Sinai tradition of the north and the David tradition of Jerusalem has been demonstrated above all by Leonhard Rost, "Sinaibund und Davidbund," *ThLZ* 72 (1947): 129–34. The division is not fully acknowledged by Antonius H. J. Gunneweg, "Sinaibund und Davidsbund," *VT* 10 (1960): 335–41. The two traditions were probably not harmonized until the Deuteronomistic era; see Niek Poulssen, *König und Tempel im Glaubenszeugnis des Alten Testaments*, SBM 3 (Stuttgart: Katholisches Bibelwerk, 1967), esp. pp. 27–142. A study must also be made of the other traditions, including the patriarchal traditions. The otherwise informative study by Klaus Seybold, *Das davidische Königtum im Zeugnis der Propheten*, FRLANT 107 (Göttingen: Vandenhoeck, 1972), suffers from the fact that it simply assumes the seamless continuity of the Sinai tradition in the Jerusalem of the early monarchy; see my review in *Bib.* 55 (1974): 93–96.
13. See Jörg Debus, *Die Sünde Jerobeams*, FRLANT 93 (Göttingen: Vandenhoeck, 1967).

12:28–32). It is possible to consider whether the verdict of the Deuteronomist is not justified in the final analysis. But it is inappropriate to the convictions of the early monarchy. The establishment of kingdom sanctuaries[14] was a political necessity. The bull images were not themselves idols but had the function of a pedestal or throne for the deity,[15] rather like the cherubim of the Jerusalem temple. High places were tolerated everywhere, at least until the reform of Josiah (622 B.C.). In the earlier period, it is likely that not all priests were Levites. Probably the Zadokite priesthood at Jerusalem in particular needed Levitical legitimation, as is done consistently in Deuteronomy. On the other hand, according to the witness of Judg. 18:30, which there is no reason to suspect, the sanctuary at Dan could trace its priesthood back to Moses.[16] The change of date for the autumn festival proves to be especially innocent, since it could not have had a fixed date at such an early period.

Did not David's transfer of the ark secure a privileged status for the Jerusalem monarchy and its temple, giving rise to corresponding convictions? This is the view of the Deuteronomist. A broad consensus of modern critical scholarship also holds that the ark brought the ancient Israelite traditions of the north to Jerusalem and made the temple the undisputed focus of the tribes. But nowhere is there any evidence of such a bond between the north and Jerusalem. Jeremiah 41:5, which is cited repeatedly, proves only that Jerusalem was then a recognized sanctuary. In addition, we are dealing with the time of the destruction of Jerusalem, preceded by more than a century of history without the Northern Kingdom. Josiah had even annexed portions of the Northern Kingdom. It is therefore unnecessary to cite the ideology of the ark to explain a certain orientation of the northern tribes toward Jerusalem. The history and significance of the ark

---

14. On this term see Amos 7:13.
15. This is the most commonly accepted view today; see Debus, *Sünde*, p. 39.
16. In the course of transmission, the name "Moses" was altered tendentiously to "Manasseh."

are much too obscure. Maier has flatly denied it the function of a bond to unify the tribes.[17] Debus, too, contests the hypothesis that the ark produced a sense of Israel as a whole.[18]

17. Johann Maier, *Das altisraelitische Ladeheiligtum*, BZAW 93 (Berlin: Töpelmann, 1965).
18. *Sünde*, pp. 41–47. According to Joseph Gutmann, "The History of the Ark," *ZAW* 83 (1971): 22–30, the Shiloh ark, which David brought to Jerusalem, is not identical with that of Josiah or the postexilic ark.

4

Nathan's Prophecy

We are still concerned with the special status of the Davidic monarchy in the convictions of the period of the monarchy. Is not the prophecy of Nathan[1] proof that the claim of the Davidic house to rule all Israel was known and largely acknowledged? It is recognized, of course, that there can be no question of explicit messianism; but the prophecy of Nathan is seen as the Magna Charta of the Davidic monarchy, fixed and effectual since the days of David, impressively documenting its monopoly on legitimacy.

Beyond question, there was a historical Nathan prophecy. At least one scholar, using literary criticism, has claimed to find it in 2 Sam. 7:11b, 16.[2] Its content would be limited to the assurance that the Davidic dynasty would endure forever; the association with the building of the temple would be a later expansion. Other scholars reject the attempt to isolate a historical nucleus and date the entire text—apart from minor Deuteronomistic interpolations—in the age of David and Solomon, most likely in the time of Solomon.[3] Their argument runs as follows: As a usurper, Solo-

---

1. The prophecy is found in 2 Samuel 7 and (dependently) in 1 Chronicles 17. The theme is also treated in Psalms 89 and 132.
2. Leonhard Rost, *Die Überlieferung von der Thronnachfolge Davids*, BWANT, ser. 3, vol. 6 (Stuttgart: Kohlhammer, 1926), reprinted in his *Das kleine Credo und andere Studien zum Alten Testament* (Heidelberg: Quelle, 1965), pp. 119–253.
3. See above all Martin Noth, "David und Israel in 2. Samuel 7," in *Mélanges bibliques rédigés en l'honneur de André Robert*, TICP 4 (Paris: Bloud, 1957, pp. 122–30, reprinted in his *Gesammelte Studien*, 1:334–45; Artur Weiser, "Die Tempelbaukrise under David," ZAW 77 (1965): 155–68; idem, "Die Legitimation des Königs David," VT 16 (1966): 325–54; Seybold, *Königtum*, pp. 26–45.

mon needed legitimation. The Nathan prophecy proved useful to him because it combined the building of the temple with a dynastic promise; as builder of the temple, he could demonstrate that he was the successor to David foreseen by Nathan. A further argument is form-critical in nature. The formal elements of the Egyptian "royal novella" have been discovered in 2 Samuel 7.[4] This is a form of Egyptian historiography, attested from the Middle Kingdom to the late period, in which institutions and regulations (for example, the building of a temple) are traced back to a decree of the king. The king makes known his intention before an audience of dignitaries; they raise objections. A certain formal similarity to 2 Samuel 7 is unmistakable. It helps to demonstrate that the text of the Nathan prophecy is a unified whole. Above all, these observations provide evidence for the date of composition: If Egyptian influence is involved, it cannot be earlier than the time of Solomon.

Apart from these considerations of literary criticism and traditio-historical criticism, the prophecy of Nathan is viewed as a legitimation document existing since the beginning of the Davidic monarchy, referred to at the enthronement of the later Davidic rulers. This explains the stability of the Davidic dynasty in contrast to the ad hoc designation of kings by prophets in the Northern Kingdom. In the south it had been determined once and for all to whom Yahweh entrusted the kingdom.

The prophecy of Nathan as a legitimation document has also been associated with the Egyptian royal protocol, which was given to the pharaoh at his enthronement in the name of the deity. It gave expression to the king's divine sonship and contained his throne name. The difference is that the Davidic kings possessed a permanent royal protocol of the dynasty.[5]

---

4. This form was first identified here by Siegfried Herrmann, "Die Königsnovelle in Ägypten und Israel," *WZ(L).GS* 3 (1953/54): 51–62. Harsh criticism of the application of the "royal novella" to 2 Samuel 7 has been leveled by Ernst Kutsch, "Die Dynastie von Gottes Gnaden," *ZThK* 58 (1961): 137–53, esp. 151ff.

5. Especially influential has been Gerhard von Rad, "The Royal Ritual in Judah," in his *The Problem of the Hexateuch and Other Essays*, trans. E. W. T. Dicken (Edinburgh: Oliver, 1966), pp. 222–31. Hans-Joachim Kraus,

As evidence for the existence of a royal protocol in Judah, the following passages may be cited: 2 Sam. 7:9, 14 (a "great name" and divine sonship); Isa. 9:5 (Eng. 9:6) (divine birth and throne names); Ps. 2:7 (divine sonship and explicit reference to the protocol with the term $hōq$, "decree"); and above all the account in 2 Kings 11:12: "Then he brought out the king's son, and put the crown upon him, and gave him the testimony (*'ēdût*)." The term *'ēdût* was previously understood as referring to the law, or else emended to *'eṣ'ādâ*, "armlet," on the basis of 2 Sam. 1:10. Egyptian texts that mention crown and royal protocol together have convinced many exegetes that 2 Kings 11:12 must refer to the royal protocol. All in all, we may consider it proved that something like a royal protocol was used at the enthronement of the kings of Judah. The conclusion that the passages refer to the prophecy of Nathan is something else again.

What can be said about the historicity of the Nathan prophecy? Rost's attempt to determine its original form by means of literary criticism may be passed over. In any case, the present text of 2 Samuel 7 cannot date from the time of Solomon; its language, ideas, and historico-theological purpose are too plainly those of the Deuteronomist. When we examine the Deuteronomistic History (Chapter 8), we shall see that the Deuteronomist makes the prophecy of Nathan the key passage for his own specific royalist expectations. The harmonization of what had originally been independent Israelite traditions in 2 Samuel 7 points to the Deuter-

---

Die Königsherrschaft Gottes im Alten Testament, BHTh 13 (Tübingen: Mohr, 1951), considers 2 Samuel 6–7 to be the festival legend of a pre-exilic "royal Zion festival," whose cultic poetry includes Psalms 89 and 132. With this theory he finds a very strong influence of the Nathan prophecy on tradition, with its locus in the cult. E. Lipiński, *Le poème royal du Psaume LXXXIX, 1–5, 20–38*, CRB 6 (Paris: Gabalda, 1967), considers the nucleus of Psalm 89 to be a propaganda document in favor of the Davidic dynasty, composed toward the end of the tenth century and already alluding to the prophecy of Nathan (see my review in *Bib.* 49 [1968]: 275–280). Critical voices have also made themselves heard on the subject of a royal protocol: According to G. H. Jones, "The Decree of Yahweh (Ps. II 7), *VT* 15 (1965): 336–44, $hōq$ in Ps. 2:7 means not just "protocol" but also "demand, ordinance." Bruno Volkwein, "Masoretisches 'ēdūt, 'ēdwōt, 'ēdōt—'Zeugnis' oder 'Bundesbestimmung'?" *BZ*, n.f. 13 (1969): 18–40, esp. 27–31, rejects the meaning "protocol" for *'ēdût* in 2 Kings 11:12, suggesting instead the meaning "covenant ordinance."

onomistic era.[6] This harmonization appears, for example, in the transformation of the promise to David into a covenant between Yahweh and David.[7] David is represented as the vassal of Yahweh. The following may be identified as elements of the ancient Near Eastern vassal treaties: the mention of earlier favors performed by the liege lord (2 Sam. 7:8–11), the "great name" (v. 9), the guarantee of security for the people provided by the liege lord (v. 10), and the dynastic promise itself. The ancient Near Eastern vassal treaties contain instances of the assurance that the vassal's descendants will continue to reign. In addition, the father-son relationship (v. 14; see also Ps. 89:27 [Eng. v. 26]) is a demonstrable element of the vassal treaties, expressing the relationship between the liege lord and his vassal.[8] But the notion of Yahweh's covenant with David appears traditio-historically to be borrowed from the Sinai tradition, which is not yet known to Isaiah, who is steeped in the traditions of Jerusalem. The passages mentioning the Davidic covenant are all late.[9] Harmonization of the Sinai covenant and the Davidic covenant like that found in 2 Samuel 7 is unlikely in the time of Solomon.

How far the Deuteronomistic redaction of 2 Samuel 7 extends

---

6. See above, Chapter 3, note 12.

7. See Roland de Vaux, "The King of Israel, Vassal of Yahweh," in his *The Bible and the Ancient Near East,* trans. D. McHugh (Garden City: Doubleday, 1971), pp. 152–66; Philip J. Calderone, *Dynastic Oracle and Suzerainty Treaty,* Logos, 1 (Manila: Loyola, 1966) (see my review in *Bib.* 50 [1969]: 111–15).

8. Despite the reservations already expressed by Dennis J. McCarthy, "Note on the Love of God in Deuteronomy and the Father-Son Relationship between Yahweh and Israel," *CBQ* 27 (1965): 144–47, see Lipiński, *Poème,* pp. 57–66; Frank C. Fensham, "Father and Son as Terminology for Treaty and Covenant," in *Near Eastern Studies in Honor of William Foxwell Albright,* ed. H. Goedicke (Baltimore: Johns Hopkins, 1971), pp. 121–35. A further biblical instance is 2 Kings 16:7. It turns out that the statements of royal sonship in Ps. 2:7 (Eng. v. 6); Isa. 9:5 (Eng. v. 6); and Ps. 110:3 (?) are different in nature, and 2 Sam. 7:14 must be dropped from the list of evidence for a royal protocol. (Similarly, the interpretation of *'ēdût* mentioned in note 5, above, for 2 Kings 11:12 would prohibit identification of this term with *ḥōq,* "royal protocol," in Ps. 2:7 [Eng. v. 6]).

9. See 2 Sam. 23:5; 2 Chron. 13:5; 21:7; Ps. 89:4, 29, 35, 40 (Eng. vv. 3, 28, 34, 39); 132:12; Jer. 33:21; also Isa. 55:3 and 2 Chron. 6:42, where instead of *bᵉrît,* "covenant," we find the synonym *ḥesed,* "grace, favor." At best, 2 Sam. 23:5 might provide evidence for the earlier period; but this passage, too, appears to be of later date.

can be seen from the fact that Nathan recites a recapitulation of sacral history and proclaims his reservations about the building of the temple as though he were the Deuteronomist in person. The historical Nathan probably was a stranger to Israelite traditions. He was presumably of Jebusite origin; in the dispute over who should succeed David (1 Kings 1–2), he supported the non-Israelite element, namely Bathsheba, the priest Zadok, and Benaiah, the leader of the mercenaries. On the other side stood the priest Abiathar from Shiloh and Joab, the leader of the militia. Ahlström,[10] who thinks Nathan was a Jebusite, traces his original opposition to the building of the temple back to his Jebusite roots, as though he wished to prevent the construction of a temple that would compete with the Jebusite sanctuary. The attitude of the *biblical* Nathan, however, is really that of the Deuteronomist.

Leaving aside the Deuteronomistic redaction of 2 Samuel 7, is it nevertheless not possible that the historical prophecy of Nathan was a permanent royal protocol of the Davidic dynasty? The fact that the Deuteronomist assigns it great importance with respect to the objectives of his work argues against this hypothesis. It is the permanent role of the prophecy that must be charged to the account of the Deuteronomist. The historical prophecy of Nathan probably remained within the framework of the usual legitimating activity of prophets and priests in the ancient Near East. The extrabiblical parallels even include an occasional dynastic promise.[11] In this case, however, we would expect that besides the oracle of Nathan there were other legitimation texts composed for each occasion, which did not have the

---

10. Gösta W. Ahlström, "Der Prophet Nathan und der Tempelbau," *VT* 11 (1961): 113–27.

11. For example, "Your son, your grandson will exercise the royal power on the knees of the god Ninurta" (James B. Pritchard, ed., *Ancient Near Eastern Texts*, 2d ed. [Princeton: Princeton University Press, 1955], p. 450; Hugo Gressmann, ed., *Altorientalische Texte und Bilder zum Alten Testament*, 2d ed. [Berlin: De Gruyter, 1926–27], 1:283; "After I [Esarhaddon] had completed that house [a temple] . . . I caused Sin, Ningal, Shamash, and Aa, the great gods, my lords, to dwell in it. . . . Therefore may Sin and Shamash . . . together constantly answer me [in oracles] . . . with offspring, with many progeny" (Kutsch, "Dynastie," p. 148).

good fortune to be played up by a Deuteronomistic author. There are several facts that conflict with the claim to uniqueness of a permanently functioning Nathan prophecy. In 2 Samuel 24 we find a temple legend that knows nothing of the prophecy of Nathan. In 2 Sam. 23:1–7, the permanence of David's dynasty is revealed to him through personal prophetic experience without the intervention of Nathan. According to Fohrer,[12] the account of Solomon's dream at Gibeon (1 Kings 3:4–15) is intended to legitimize the king; there is no reference to the prophecy of Nathan. The same is true in a series of texts that can be understood as the products of legitimation at court: Isa. 8:23—9:6 (Eng. 9:1–7); 11:1–5; Psalms 2; 45; 110; for the moment we may ignore the question of whether these texts directly or indirectly reflect an enthronement ceremony.[13] For 2 Kings 11:12, too, it cannot be proven that the "testimony" (*'ēdût*)—if we are in fact dealing with a royal protocol—refers to the prophecy of Nathan. Passages like 1 Sam. 13:13–14; 25:28, 30; 2 Sam. 3:9, 18; 5:2; 1 Chron. 11:3 may have been composed by the historiographer as part of the framework of the total narrative but presuppose that repeated acts of legitimation were customary.

If we have reduced the historical prophecy of Nathan to more modest dimensions, this does not mean that the Deuteronomist had no historical basis for his larger-than-life-size description. When all is said and done, Nathan did legitimize the great king whose dynasty was to endure for a significant length of time. The sense of legitimation may well have been especially highly developed in the case of David and Solomon, as is true of all powerful rulers. This notion may be expressed architecturally in the temple columns Jachin and Boaz (1 Kings 7:21).[14] It has only

---

12. Georg Fohrer, "Der Vertrag zwischen König und Volk in Israel," *ZAW* 71 (1953): 1–22.

13. See Becker, *Isaias*, pp. 22–29; on Psalm 45, see Joachim Becker, *Israel deutet seine Psalmen*, SBS 18 (Stuttgart: Katholisches Bibelwerk, 1966), pp. 80–90.

14. See Robert B. Y. Scott, "The Pillars Jachin and Boaz," *JBL* 58 (1939): 143–49; Walter Kornfeld, "Der Symbolismus der Tempelsäulen," *ZAW* 74 (1962): 50–57. Scott even finds in their names the incipits of legitimation formulas whose wording can be reconstructed on the basis of 2 Sam. 7:13 and Ps. 21:2 (Eng. v. 1).

been our purpose to protect against the serious error of cloaking an interpretation on the part of the Deuteronomist in the guise of critical history and ascribing to the Davidic monarchy a special status that it did not enjoy in the eyes of contemporaries.

5

The Yahwist

There are two reasons why the Yahwist's history must be considered independently. First, we should avoid the possibility that a single pro-Judah author, who plays a dominant role in the Old Testament, might through his attitude toward the Davidic monarchy lend support to a historical overestimate like that of the Deuteronomistic History, especially the prophecy of Nathan. Second, we have an opportunity to examine the "messianic" texts Gen. 49:8–12 and Num. 24:15–24, which serve to bridge the patriarchal and Mosaic periods in the traditional picture of messianic expectation, and evaluate them historically. It leads to exaggerated interpretations when they are treated like precious jewels and isolated from the interpretive context of a literary composition and its historical background.

We shall not even attempt to prove that the two passages belong to the Yahwistic history. Neither can we go into the differences of opinion concerning the nature and date of this work. The question of its date is especially onerous. Since the work provides a finished synthesis of all Israelite traditions, it cannot have been composed during the period of Solomon or shortly thereafter. The argument from its religio-political mood, which emphasizes joy in national existence and magnanimity toward other nations while at the same time favoring the monarchy, is much too vague. The idea of the Davidic empire could be a vital influence in a later period.[1] Koch[2] proposes the important theory

---

1. See John Mauchline, "Implicit Signs of a Persistent Belief in the Davidic Empire," VT 20 (1970): 287–303.
2. Klaus Koch, "Die Hebräer vom Auszug aus Ägypten bis zum Grossreich Davids," VT 19 (1969): 37–81, esp. 71–81.

of a Hebrew ideology on the part of the Yahwist in which is reflected the assimilation of Edom, Moab, Ammon, Ishmael, and Aram into the Davidic empire; but this theory is not a conclusive argument for an early date. With respect to the disputed question of whether the work extends beyond (Numbers and) Joshua into the books of Samuel and Kings, we are inclined toward a positive answer. The evaluation of the Davidic monarchy would then rest on a broader foundation. But even in the case of the shorter answer, which we must take as our point of departure, the idea of the Davidic empire is detectable.

Within the context of the Yahwistic history, Gen. 49:8–12 and Num. 24:15–24 are fictive prophecies of the Davidic monarchy. We therefore firmly reject the attempt of the religio-historical school to demonstrate the existence of an explicit expectation of a savior in the premonarchic period.[3] It is commonly held today that the monarchy does not belong to the nucleus of the Yahwist's kerygma.[4] According to Ruppert, the central theme is the leading of mankind to salvation; according to Wolff, it is the history of the blessing given Abraham, so that Wolff logically finds the conclusion of the work in the blessing of Balaam. In any case, after the story of how humankind brought disaster upon themselves has been told, a turning point that looks toward salvation appears in Gen. 12:1–3. It is conceivable that the idea of the Davidic empire serves as the goal. Under David, Israel was the "great nation" foreseen in Gen. 12:2; and the "great name" of Gen. 12:2 recalls 2 Sam. 7:9 (and 8:13). The correspondence would be especially convincing if the passages in the Book of Samuel came from the pen of the Yahwist. The Yahwist has in mind the notion that Israel is assigned a mission with respect to the nations

3. See Ernst Sellin, *Die israelitisch-jüdische Heilandserwartung*, BZSF, ser. 5, vols. 2–3 (Berlin: Runge, 1909); idem, "Zu dem Judaspruch im Jacobsegen Gen 49,8–12 und im Mosesegen Deut 33,7," ZAW 66 (1944): 57–67; Lorenz Dürr, *Ursprung und Ausbau der israelitisch-jüdischen Heilandserwartung* (Berlin: Schwetschke, 1925); Hugo Gressmann, *Der Messias*, FRLANT 43 (Göttingen: Vandenhoeck, 1929).

4. See Hans Walter Wolff, "Das Kerygma des Jahwisten," *EvTh* 24 (1964): 73–98, reprinted in his *Gesammelte Studien zum Alten Testament*, TB 22, 2d ed. (Munich: Kaiser, 1973), pp. 345–73; Lothar Ruppert, "Der Jahwist—Künder der Heilsgeschichte," in *Wort und Botschaft*, ed. J. Schreiner (Würzburg: Echter, 1967), pp. 88–107; Koch, "Hebräer."

brought together in the empire of David; that is confirmed by the Hebrew ideology outlined by Koch. It is true that if this is the goal pointed to by the opening act of salvation described by the Yahwist in Gen. 12:1–3, it appears rather narrow and banally political in comparison with the universal human perspective of Genesis 1–11. But it is possible that the Yahwist viewed the curse imposed on humankind as having been removed by the blessing of the Davidic empire. He himself lives in expectation that this empire will be restored. In the course of his presentation, he judges the nations by their conduct toward Israel; they must recognize the blessing of Abraham.[5] But none of the Yahwist's passages that speak of a blessing refers explicitly to the Davidic monarchy. Such a reference appears only in the saying concerning Judah in Gen. 49:8–12 and the fourth oracle of Balaam, Num. 24:15–24.

We do not wish to enter into the discussion as to whether victory over the curse upon humankind is already proclaimed in Gen. 3:15. To the extent that this claim can be demonstrated, this passage, too, must be interpreted in the context of the Yahwist's kerygma. If we start from the position that the Yahwist sees the curse as having been overcome through the position of Israel as a great power, the victory of the woman and her descendants over the serpent must also be associated with the mission of Israel. This does not mean that the "seed of the woman" in Gen. 3:15 refers to David in person; the perspective of the verse is too much that of human etiology for this to be so. It is not David who overcomes the serpent; rather, the curse that is ultimately expressed in enmity with the serpent is overcome by the plenitude of blessing supplied by the glory of the Israelite empire. It is even less possible for the Yahwist to have pictured the "seed of the woman" as a messianic figure. Spinetoli[6] has supported this view, arguing that the Yahwist was influenced by the messianic

---

5. See Gen. 12:3; 27:29; Num. 24:9. Other passages in which the blessing of Abraham is spoken of or takes effect include Gen. 18:17ff.; 22:18; 26:4, 24; 26:12ff. (compare v. 28); 28:14; 30:27; 39:5; Exod. 12:32.

6. Ortensio da Spinetoli, "La data e l'interpretazione del protovangelo (Gen. 3,15)," in *Il Messianismo*, 18th Settimana Biblica of the Associazione Biblica Italiana (Brescia: Paideia, 1966), pp. 35–56.

movement expressed in Isaiah 7–11 and Micah 5. His methodology is correct in that Gen. 3:15 must be interpreted consistently within the context of the Yahwist's kerygma. But a preexilic messianic movement is an untenable hypothesis. Only the Septuagint, which uses the masculine form *autòs* to refer to the neuter *spérma,* could have interpreted the woman's seed messianically.[7]

There is no need for a detailed discussion of the individual problems associated with Gen. 49:8–12.[8] In any case, the preeminence of the tribe of Judah is fictively predicted. A precise understanding of the disputed verse 49:10 must decide whether the statement—as we would expect in a tribal saying—singles out only the tribe as such (albeit with David in mind), or whether, as in Num. 24:17, there is an allusion to the person of David. The crux is the clause "until *šílōh* comes." Whoever would find a reference to the person of the ruler must emend the Masoretic *šílōh*.[9] Exegetes who favor nothing more than a statement concerning the tribe also sometimes resort to textual emendation.[10] But they can also read the Masoretic text as it stands, which obviously mentions the city of Shiloh ("until it [the tribe of Judah] comes to Shiloh"). Elsewhere the name of the ancient Israelite sanctuary is spelled *šylw, šlh,* or *šlw;* but the

---

7. See Raymond A. Martin, "The Earliest Messianic Interpretation of Genesis 3:15," *JBL* 84 (1965): 425–27.

8. See Hans-Peter Müller, "Zur Frage nach dem Ursprung der biblischen Eschatologie," *VT* 14 (1964): 276–93; Hans Jürgen Zobel, *Stammesspruch und Geschichte,* BZAW 95 (Berlin: Töpelmann, 1965), pp. 10–15, 72–80; Rehm, *Der königliche Messias,* pp. 16–23; supplementing the material in Rehm, see B. Margulis, "Gen. XLIX 10 / Deut. XXXIII 2–3," *VT* 19 (1969): 202–10; Liudger Sabottka, "Noch einmal Gen. 49,10," *Bib.* 51 (1970): 225–29; B. Margulis, "Emendation and Exegesis: A Reply to L. Sabottka," *Bib.* 51 (1971): 226–28.

9. Examples include: *šellōh,* "to whom it appertains (ancient versions); *šēlu,* "prince, ruler" (the Akkadian word, recognized today as a ghost word); *mōšᵉlōh,* "its ruler"; *šᵉʾilōh,* "its desired one"; *šālûaḥ,* "the one to be sent" (Vulgate); *šālēw,* "the peaceful one"; "to you will come the son of Jesse" (the venturesome translation of Margulis).

10. Examples include: *šay lōh,* "tribute to him" (in other words, until tribute comes or is brought to him); *šellōh,* in the sense "what appertains to it" (in other words, until there comes what appertains to it [the tribe of Judah]; this is the reading of most manuscripts of the Septuagint and Theodotion).

form *šylh* that appears in Gen. 49:10 is attested as a reading in Ps. 78:60 by many manuscripts and is therefore unobjectionable. A material difficulty is raised by the fact that Shiloh is generally held to have been destroyed by the Philistines toward the end of the period of the Judges. Perhaps, however, the sanctuary was still in existence until the events of 732 or 721/22 B.C. (see Judg. 18:31). What the Yahwist actually means by "coming to Shiloh" remains obscure. At any event, a claim to hegemony on the part of Judah is expressed.[11]

The fourth oracle of Balaam (Num. 24:15-24) is assigned convincingly to the Yahwistic source document.[12] Typically Yahwistic is the discussion of the fates of the various nations. The prediction with respect to Moab and Edom is fulfilled in 2 Sam. 8:2, 13-14. The "star out of Jacob" (v. 17) probably refers directly to the person of David.[13]

---

11. See Rehm, *Der königliche Messias*, p. 19, n. 69. Not all authors connect the Shiloh claim of Judah with the Davidic empire, even when the text is not emended. Zobel, for example, finds in verses 10–12 an interpretive passage from the late period of the Judges and interprets verses 11–12, which probably do express a fullness of blessing, somewhat strangely as referring to the brutal arrival of the tribe of Judah at Shiloh. Sabottka's conjecture, "his throne (*'ad*) will truly come to Shiloh," is not convincing but does not touch the salient point.

12. Walter Gross, *Bileam*, StANT 38 (Munich: Kösel, 1974) considers the presence of the Yahwistic source in Numbers 22–24 unlikely. For bibliography on the oracle of Balaam, see Rehm, *Der königliche Messias*, pp. 23–29, and additional bibliography in Klaus Seybold, "Das Herrscherbild des Bileamorakels Num. 24,15–19," *ThZ* 29 (1973): 1–19.

13. William F. Albright, "The Oracles of Balaam (Num. 22–23)," *JBL* 63 (1944): 207–33; Albright dates the oracle in the premonarchic period but is forced to eliminate the reference to David by textual emendation: "When the stars of Jacob triumph and the tribes of Israel rise. . . ."

6

Sacral Kingship and Messianism during the Monarchy

Since we are coming to a crucial phase of our historical presentation, it is appropriate to summarize our conclusions up to this point. In the premonarchic period, Israel's sociological composition made it antimonarchic. Genesis 49:8–12 and Num. 24:15–24 are fictive predictions (*vaticinia ex eventu*) of a later writer, the Yahwist, who has the Davidic empire before his eyes. The monarchy begins without at first being integrated into the ideology of Yahwism. Traditio-historically, it leads a kind of separate existence at the royal courts. In the historical conviction of the period of the monarchy, the Davidic monarchy did not enjoy a special status in sacral history. The sense of legitimation at the royal court of Jerusalem does not in principle go beyond the usual limits found elsewhere in the ancient Near East.

Against this background, we can ask whether there was a messianic expectation in the period of the monarchy. Passages deserving serious consideration include Isa. 7:10–16 (and 8:8); 8:23—9:6 (Eng. 9:1–7); 11:1–5; Mic. 5:1–5 (Eng. vv. 2–6); Psalms 2, 45, 72, 110. Other royal psalms (Psalms 18, 20, 21, 101, 144) are usually not considered messianic; Psalms 89 and 132 might be considered messianic at most in the indirect sense of the Nathan prophecy, whose themes they incorporate. Hosea 3:5 and Amos 9:11 derive from exilic or postexilic redaction.

Modern critical exegesis understands these texts totally within their own historical context and therefore does not impute to them, as it were, a visionary preview of Christ. It nevertheless seeks to find a messianic element in them to the extent that they express an expectation of a future royal savior. Such an expectation is not eschatological in the same sense as the "imminent eschatology" of the exilic and postexilic period, and certainly not in the same sense as the transcendental eschatology of late Jewish apocalypticism. We might speak of a "protoeschatology" that studies the horizons of its own age.

We find no good reason for any concession—possibly unconscious—to the naive messianic interpretation espoused by tradition, and we consider the following methodological approach desirable. It is certain that there was no widespread movement involving messianic expectations. Geographically, the texts refer only to the Southern Kingdom, and of the prophets only Isaiah and Micah are involved. In the historical preaching of Hosea and Amos, there is no trace of any royal expectation looking to the future. Neither is any to be found in Zephaniah, a prophet in the Southern Kingdom during the time of Josiah, or in Nahum and Habakkuk. But the scattered texts—of which only those in Isaiah appear to be preexilic—can be understood plausibly against the background of sacral kingship or royal ideology and bear the stamp of the particular circle surrounding the Jerusalem court prophet Isaiah. A preexilic messianism is almost a contradiction in terms, since the savior king is in fact present. We consider messianic texts appearing suddenly out of the blue to be questionable and seek to read them against their own historical background. We shall find this perspective confirmed in the exilic and postexilic situation. Nowhere do we find that the immediate historical possibilities are transcended.

There is nothing to prevent claiming that the texts that draw on royal ideology are messianic in a broader sense. They express the yearning of humanity for an ideal king, fulfilled in Christ. But since it is our task to inquire into the historical convictions lying in the foreground, it remains true that they are not messianic in the usual sense. In addition, they exhibit features of a kingship that is most closely analogous to our conception of messianism, which we judge by the criterion of Christ, the sacral king par excellence. No wonder there seems to be justification for imputing a visionary description of the kingship of Christ to these passages. Historical examination must reach a far different conclusion. Sacral kingship was especially suspect to Yahwism, which had a hard enough time with kingship in general. While kingship as an institution was ultimately integrated, features of royal ideology were interpreted away. They survived only in scattered texts, and even there (as we shall see in Chapter 11) only by virtue of reinterpretation. From the perspective of New Testament fulfillment, they represent dead ends in the economy of salvation.

There is no need here for a detailed description of sacral kingship in the ancient Near East and the pertinent scholarship. This has been the domain of the myth and ritual school (sometimes called the London school) and a series of important Scandinavian exegetes.[1] A few typical features will suffice for our purpose. The sacral king is a bearer of blessing. In the ritual of "sacral marriage" at the New Year festival he guarantees the fertility of the coming year. He is the representative of the people, whom, as it were, he conceals within himself. At the same time, he is the representative, indeed the "incarnation," of the deity, of whom he is begotten as "son of god."[2] Whether his sonship is to be understood physically or in a metaphorical sense is of lesser importance. The sacral king functions as a priest at major cultic events.

It is of crucial importance whether ideas associated with this royal ideology were operative in preexilic Israel, more particularly in Jerusalem. Only if this is the case do the conditions obtain for our explanation of the supposedly messianic passages.

---

1. For the most important literature, see Joachim Becker, *Wege der Psalmenexegese*, SBS 78 (Stuttgart: Katholisches Bibelwerk, 1975), pp. 38–48.

2. Several extensive Egyptian texts with bibliographical references may be found in Manfred Görg, "Die 'Wiedergeburt' des Königs (Ps. 2,7b)," ThGl 60 (1971): 413–26, esp. 417–21; see also idem, *Gott-König-Reden in Israel und Ägypten*, BWANT 6/5 (Stuttgart: Kohlhammer, 1975).

The state of scholarship on this point is extraordinarily confused. One important school of thought[3] maintains on the basis of the sources that Israelite kingship was definitely *not* sacral, and minimizes the pertinent evidence. Scholars belonging to the London and Scandinavian schools mentioned above, on the contrary, sometimes exhibit no restraint in applying to Israel the ancient Near Eastern ideas of sacral kingship, which themselves do not form a uniform whole.[4] This vexing instance of a fundamental difference of exegetical opinion is due to divergent assessments of the Old Testament sources. While the former group concedes to the historical books a historically accurate picture of Israelite kingship, which exhibits none of the features of royal ideology, the latter is convinced that certain realities have been consciously concealed. This group distinguishes between the Old Testament as a catch basin where conceptions were purified and interpreted and the actual religious ideas and institutions of the historical Israel. We agree with the scholars who are oriented toward the royal ideology that Old Testament historiography cannot be taken at face value, but we wish to point out that the existence of sacral kingship does not stand or fall with the occasionally exaggerated interpretations of the schools just mentioned.[5]

The nature of the evidence that suggests that the Israelite kings exercised the functions of sacral kingship can only be sketched in outline. The cultic abuses castigated by the prophets, behind which we may look for Canaanite fertility cults, did not halt at the gates of the royal courts. Someone like Ahaz (2 Kings 16:3–4) or Manasseh (2 Kings 21:6), who offered their sons as a sacrifice, is psychologically close to the fertility ritual of the "sacral marriage." In Lam. 4:20, the king is called the breath of life of his people; before the exile, such an expression could have had a fuller ideological background. The description in Ezek. 8:3, 5,

---

3. Represented, for instance, by Albrecht Alt and Martin Noth (see the studies cited above in Chapter 3, note 8), and de Fraine, *L'aspect religieux.*

4. The biblical data are utilized especially strikingly by Geo Widengren, *Sakrales Königtum im Alten Testament und im Judentum,* FDV, 1952 (Stuttgart: Kohlhammer, 1955).

5. For a comprehensive critical discussion, see Bernhardt, *Problem.*

14-15 is informative. The priesthood of the kings has been thoroughly eliminated from the Old Testament, which admits as priests only Levites in the Deuteronomistic literature, and later only the sons of Aaron.[6] But the king was still lord of the temple and leader of the cult. The sons of David are called priests in 2 Sam. 8:18, and the Chronicler found it necessary to alter this statement to make it inoffensive (1 Chron. 18:17). The going in and out of the priest before Yahweh's anointed (1 Sam. 2:35) vividly depicts the subordination of the priest to the king. It is possible that Moses is described after the manner of the preexilic lord of the temple when he installs Aaron as priest. The Deuteronomistic history, to which notions of sacral kingship are alien, recounts the performance of cultic acts by kings, such as sacrifice and blessing.[7] The Chronicler later engages in guerrilla warfare, attacking this picture with the help of clever manipulation of the text.[8] The Chronicler even takes into account the position of the king in the temple and removes him from the altar by seeking at least to obscure the situation.[9] The polemic against the association of the king with the cult is even stronger in the Book of Ezekiel.[10] Before the exile the royal palace was connected with the sanctuary, so that the temple has been referred to (exaggeratedly) as the royal chapel of the Davidic kings. But the palace is totally omitted from the temple plan in Ezekiel 40ff. The king may participate in the cult at the head of the people, but he may no longer enter the inner court (Ezek. 44:1-3; 46:1-12). The vigorous polemic of the Chronicler and the Book of Ezekiel is eloquent. Before the exile, there was much that differed from what

---

6. This point is minimized by Jean de Fraine, "Peut-on parler d'un véritable sacerdoce du roi en Israël?" in *Sacra pagina*, ed. J. Coppens, BEThL 12-13 (Gembloux: Duculot, 1959), 1:537-47.

7. See, for example, 2 Sam. 6:18; 1 Kings 8:55ff.; 12:32; 13:1; 2 Kings 16:12-13.

8. See Poulssen, *König*, pp. 155-59. In 2 Chron. 26:16-20 (which has no equivalent in the Books of Kings), the Chronicler is obviously conducting a polemic against the sacrificial office of the king.

9. See ibid., pp. 159-66. Compare 1 Kings 8:22 with its parallel 2 Chron. 6:12-13; 2 Kings 11:14 with 2 Chron. 23:13; 2 Kings 23:3 with 2 Chron. 23:31; note also 2 Chron. 20:5 (no equivalent in Kings).

10. See ibid., pp. 148-50.

the Old Testament would like to see true. One theory, which has never been disproved, sees in the vestments of the postexilic high priest, in his anointing, and in certain cultic functions (for example, the great Day of Atonement of Leviticus 16) an echo of royal institutions of the preexilic period.[11] The kings seem in truth to have been "priests forever after the order of Melchizedek" (Ps. 110:4).

Does the anointing of the king[12] also constitute part of the sacral kingship? The ancient Near Eastern evidence is unexpectedly scanty. There is no evidence at all for anointing in Mesopotamia; the Egyptian pharaoh was not anointed at his enthronement. But the kings of the Hittites were anointed; and according to Amarna Letter 51, vassal kings were anointed by the pharaoh as a sign of the transfer of honor and power. Kutsch proposes the theory that the anointing of the kings of Israel was due to Hittite influence. According to him, this anointing was understood not as communicating honor and power but as a purely juridical act, a well-attested feature in the ancient Near East. In Israel, only the anointing by the people is historical, not anointing by a priest or prophet on behalf of Yahweh. On the basis of this theory, Kutsch denies that the postexilic anointing of the high priest, which signifies a communicated consecration, is the successor to the preexilic anointing of the king. Anointing was not customary in the case of the northern kings. The term "anointed of Yahweh," according to Kutsch, does not presuppose an actual anointing.[13] Richter[14] attempts to extract from 1 Samuel 9–10 a *nāgîd* anointing of charismatic military leaders during the period of the Judges, transferred to the monarchy from the time

---

11. See especially Widengren, *Sakrales Königtum,* pp. 17–33.
12. See Mowinckel, *He That Cometh,* pp. 3–8; de Vaux, *Ancient Israel,* pp. 103–6; idem, "Roi d'Israel"; Ernst Kutsch, *Salbung als Rechtsakt im Alten Testament und im alten Orient,* BZAW 87 (Berlin: Töpelmann, 1963); Schmidt, *Menschlicher Erfolg,* pp. 172–88.
13. Kutsch also denies the historicity of the anointing of prophets attested directly or indirectly in 1 Kings 19:15–16; Ps. 105:15; Isa. 61:1 (see also CD ii. 12 and 1QM xi. 7).
14. *Richterbuch,* pp. 288–93; the same theory is espoused in Richter's studies cited above in Chapter 3, note 7.

of David. Contrary to Kutsch and Richter, Schmidt[15] reaffirms the traditional view that anointing was borrowed from the Canaanites along with kingship. This alone can account for the number of times it is mentioned as a matter of course.[16] Royal anointing is by nature sacral, but it may have seemed relatively unobjectionable to orthodox Yahwism. This would explain the success of the expression *māšîaḥ yahweh*, "Yahweh's anointed." Absolute usage (*"the* anointed," *"the* messiah") does not appear in the Old Testament.

This sketch of the possibility of finding ideas associated with sacral kingship in the preexilic period is intended to prepare us for encountering statements intensely expressive of royal ideology in Ps. 2:7 ("You are my son, today I have begotten you"), Ps. 45:7 (Eng. v. 6) ("Your throne, O God, endures for ever and ever"),[17] Ps. 110:3 ("With you is princely dominion from the day of your birth in holy splendor; from the womb of the morning you have the dew of your sonship"),[18] and Isa. 9:5 (Eng. v. 6)

---

15. *Menschlicher Erfolg*, pp. 172–75.
16. The act of anointing is mentioned or described with respect to Saul: 1 Sam. 9:16; 10:1; 15:1, 17; 11:15 (LXX); David: 1 Sam. 16:13; 2 Sam. 2:4, 7; 3:39; 5:3, 17; 12:7; Ps. 89:21 (Eng. v. 20); 1 Chron. 11:3; 14:8; Absalom: 2 Sam. 19:11 (Eng. v. 12); Solomon: 1 Kings 1:34, 39, 45; 5:15 (Eng. v. 1); 1 Chron. 29:22; Jehu: 1 Kings 19:16; 2 Kings 9:3, 6, 12; 2 Chron. 22:7; Joash: 2 Kings 11:12; 2 Chron. 23:11; Jehoahaz: 2 Kings 23:30; see also Ps. 45:8 (Eng. v. 7) and, for anointing outside of Israel, 1 Kings 19:15 (Hazael of Damascus). The term "Yahweh's anointed" is applied to Saul: 1 Sam. 24:7, 11 (Eng. vv. 6, 10); 26:9, 11, 16, 23; 2 Sam. 1:14, 16; David: 1 Sam. 16:6; 2 Sam. 19:22 (Eng. v. 21); 23:1; Solomon: 2 Chron. 6:42; Zedekiah: Lam. 4:20; Cyrus: Isa. 45:1; an individual not further specified: 1 Sam. 2:10, 35; 2 Sam. 22:51 (=Ps. 18:51 [Eng. v. 50]); Hab. 3:13; Ps. 2:2; 20:7 (Eng. v. 6); 28:8; 84:10 (Eng. v. 9); 89:39, 52 (Eng. vv. 38, 51); 132:10, 17.
17. For this interpretation of the text (*'ĕlōhîm*, "God," as vocative), see Bernard Couroyer, "Dieu ou Roi?" *RB* 78 (1971): 233–41. The most important alternatives are: "Your throne, like the throne of God, endures for ever and ever," and "Your throne is God's for ever and ever" (Johannes Mulder, *Studies on Psalm 45* [Oss: Witsiers, 1972]). In any case, the psalm bears the stamp of royal ideology.
18. A complete examination of the passage would fill a book. The Masoretic text can be translated: "Your people are willing on the day of your battle in holy array; from the womb of the morning the dew of your youth flows to you." In this case, there is no talk of "sonship" or "begetting."

("For to us a child is born, to us a son is given . . ."; "mighty God"). The father-son relationship mentioned in 2 Sam. 7:14 and Ps. 89:27 (Eng. v. 26) is not associated with the royal ideology.[19]

Even if the circumstantial evidence were not sufficient, the passages just cited would compel us to postulate a sacral kingship. It is debatable whether the Davidic monarchy in Jerusalem continues the pre-Israelite city monarchy without a break.[20] We may be dealing with a "regression" like the Renaissance. All that the texts require is that the ideology of sacral kingship must have been current at some time, although the city monarchy of the Davidic dynasty in Jerusalem provides a convenient point of entrance. All the evidence points to Jerusalem. The extent to which royal ideology was adapted to Yahwism is irrelevant; purely external borrowing of a few typical elements would suffice. But we must also reckon with the possibility of syncretism. It is not necessarily true that everyone found everything equally objectionable. Isaiah of Jerusalem lives in a different psychological world from that of a prophet living in the Israelite heartland. And he certainly need not share the reservations of later critics.

We cannot leave the matter without mentioning that many exegetes date the alleged evidence for a preexilic messianic expectation in the exilic or postexilic period, at least in part. Even if this is true, these passages still retain their value as evidence for the ideology of the sacral kingship in the period of the monarchy, since the exilic and postexilic authors draw their inspiration from the preexilic situation. But all further discussion of any preexilic messianic expectation would be superfluous. The late dating is very commonly accepted in the case of Psalms 2, 45, 72, and 110, and we shall follow this dating in another place.[21] But

---

In place of "in holy splendor" or "in holy array," many scholars prefer the reading "on holy mountains," clearly connected with royal ideology. The substantive *yaldutim* ("sonship" or "youth") is often emended to a verbal form ("I have begotten you"), following the Septuagint. If only because priesthood is ascribed to the king (v. 4), the psalm is still evidence for the royal ideology.

19. See above, Chapter 4, note 8.
20. See Gen. 14:18–20; Ps. 110:4. The continuity is denied by Bernhardt, *Problem*, pp. 91–102.
21. See below, Chapter 11.

the dating of Isa. 8:23—9:6 (Eng. 9:1–7); 11:1–5; and Mic. 5:1–5 is also in question. An exilic or postexilic background is in fact preferable for Mic. 5:1–5, and the postexilic reinterpretation of the two Isaiah passages also needs to be studied.[22] But there is no need to deny the historical Isaiah's authorship of the two passages. The argumentation of scholars who maintain the contrary[23] can certainly be vouched for on historical grounds. With a sharp eye for what is historically possible, they see that the messianism that they, too, (wrongly) find expressed in the texts is out of place in the preexilic period. We would reply that a present-oriented interpretation based on royal ideology provides an acceptable possibility of a setting in the ministry of the Jerusalem court prophet Isaiah.

Our historical survey must forego exegesis of the individual texts. What is important is their setting. We understand Isa. 8:23—9:6 (Eng. 9:1–7) and 11:1–5, the only passages left as preexilic evidence, as having been composed for the enthronement of a Davidic ruler. They are products of the legitimating work of a Jerusalem court prophet, who was far from preaching messianism to an esoteric circle of disciples while ignoring the kings of his own day. The enthronement setting is suggested by the reference to presentation of a scepter and the enthronement names in Isa. 9:5–6 (Eng. vv. 6–7).[24] The "birth of a child" and the "gift of a son" represent the notion of the king's being begotten by the deity on the day of his enthronement. In my opinion, Isa. 11:1–5 belongs as a compositional unit with 10:(27)28–34; it has the same setting as 8:23—9:6 (Eng. 9:1–7).[25]

---

22. Ibid.

23. See Georg Fohrer, *Das Buch Jesaja*, ZBK, 2d ed. (Zurich: Zwingli, 1966–67), vol. 1, ad loc.; Jochen Vollmer, "Zur Sprache von Jesaja 9,1–6," *ZAW* 80 (1968): 343–50; idem, "Jesajanische Begrifflichkeit?" *ZAW* 83 (1971): 389–91. Besides historical considerations, linguistic and redactional questions play a role.

24. For a discussion of the enthronement names, see (besides the material in Rehm, *Der königliche Messias*, pp. 145–66) Walter Zimmerli, "Vier oder fünf Thronnamen des messianischen Herrschers in Jes. IX 5b.6," *VT* 22 (1972): 249–52; Klaus Dietrich Schunk, "Der fünfte Thronname des Messias," *VT* 23 (1973): 108–10.

25. On these two passages in the preaching of Isaiah, see the detailed

We have taken no account of the Immanuel oracle in Isa. 7:10–16, for many the very heart of preexilic messianic expectation.[26] Kittel[27] makes the emotional statement: "The hour in which Isaiah departed from Ahaz gave to the world the idea of the Messiah." This is not true with respect to either the historical oracle of Isaiah or the redactional additions of the Book of Isaiah.[28] It is not even certain that the oracle deals with a royal

discussions in Becker, *Isaias*, esp. pp. 21–30; on the first passage, see Joachim Becker, "Jes 9,1–6 (Weihnachten 1. Messe)," in *Die alttestamentlichen Lesungen der Sonn- und Feiertage; Auslegung und Verkündigung,* ed. Josef Schreiner (Würzburg: Echter, 1969), 1:58–71. Comprehensive bibliography will be found in Rehm, *Der königliche Messias,* pp. 130–234. The interpretation of Isa. 9:5 (Eng. v. 6) as referring to the "king's birth" in the context of his enthronement received the important support of Albrecht Alt, "Jesaja 8,23—9,6," in *Festschrift Alfred Bertholet,* ed. W. Baumgartner (Tübingen: Mohr, 1950), pp. 29–49, reprinted in his *Kleine Schriften,* 2:206–25. On the enthronement setting and "king's birth" (rather than the physical birth of a child), which many still misinterpret in a messianic sense, see also Margaret B. Crook, "A Suggested Occasion for Isaiah 9:1–6 and 11:1–9," *JBL* 68 (1949): 213–24 (an enthronement ritual not composed by Isaiah; no mention of the "king's birth"); von Rad, "Royal Ritual," p. 230 (messianic); Widengren, *Sakrales Königtum,* pp. 54–56; Robert B. Y. Scott and G. G. D. Kilpatrick, "The Book of Isaiah, Chapters 1–39," in *The Interpreter's Bible,* ed. G. A. Buttrick (Nashville: Abingdon, 1956), 5:231–34; Otto Kaiser, *Isaiah 1–12,* trans. R. A. Wilson, OTL (Philadelphia: Westminster, 1972), pp. 125–30 (messianic); Claus Schedl, *History of the Old Testament* (Staten Island: Alba, 1972-1973), 4: 228, n. 60 (messianic); Siegfried Herrmann, *Die prophetischen Heilserwartungen im Alten Testament,* BWANT, ser. 5, vol. 5 (Stuttgart: Kohlhammer, 1965), pp. 132–37 (insertion by a later follower); Olegario Garcia de la Fuente, "La cronología de los reyes de Judá y la interpretación de algunos oráculos de Isaías 1–39," *EstB* 31 (1972): 275–91.

26. Most recently Rehm, *Der königliche Messias,* pp. 30–121. The following may be cited in addition to the bibliography in Rehm: Rudolf Kilian, *Die Verheissung Immanuels,* SBS 35 (Stuttgart: Katholisches Bibelwerk, 1968); idem, "Prolegomena zur Auslegung der Immanuelverheissung," in *Wort, Lied, und Gottespruch,* Festschrift J. Ziegler, ed. J. Schreiner, FzB 1–2 (Würzburg: Echter, 1972), 1:207–15; Johann Jakob Stamm, "Die Immanuelperikope im Lichte neuerer Veröffentlichungen," in 17th Deutscher Orientalistentag *Vorträge,* ed. W. Voigt, ZDMG.S 1 (Wiesbaden: Steiner, 1969), pp. 281–90; idem, "Die Immanuel-Perikope," *ThZ* 30 (1974): 11–22; Herbert M. Wolf, "A Solution to the Immanuel Prophecy in Isaiah 7:14—8:22," *JBL* 91 (1972): 449–56; Odil H. Steck, "Beiträge zum Verständnis von Jesaja 7,10–17 und 8,1–4," *ThZ* 29 (1973): 161–78.

27. Rudolf Kittel, *A History of the Hebrews,* trans. J. Taylor, H. W. Hogg, and E. B. Speirs, TTL 3, 6 (London: Williams, 1895-1896), 2:346.

28. On the redactional material, see Becker, *Isaias,* pp. 53–58, and Chapter 11, below.

figure; if so, it refers not to a messiah but to a son of Ahaz. There is a widely held alternative interpretation that deserves serious consideration, namely, that the word ʿalmâ refers to some young woman who can call her son Immanuel, "God with us," on account of the saving intervention of Yahweh. In this case no significance attaches to the person of the boy. Possibly those authors are right who take Isa. 8:1–4 as their starting point and consider Immanuel to be a son of Isaiah. No other passage illustrates so clearly how far the traditional picture of messianic expectation can depart from history.

7

Restorative Monarchism and Theocracy after the Monarchy

Had there been a tradition of messianic expectation before the Exile, it would necessarily have come to light after the end of the monarchy in 586 B.C. The expectation, free of the distracting presence of the king in the flesh, could fasten on the messianic ruler of the future. We shall therefore look for an illustration. It is well known that remarkably little interest is shown in any messianic figure. But scholarship is far from a correct appraisal of the messianological vacuum.[1] It can be surprising only to someone who has painted a false picture of messianic expectation.

In the exilic and postexilic periods, we find two tendencies that should be obvious to anyone who thinks in historical terms. As so often in history—in the case of the Bourbons and the House of Hapsburg, for example—when the monarchy came to an end there was a royalist movement devoted to hope for a restoration of the Davidic monarchy. In addition—and no less appropriate to the historical situation—we can observe a renunciation of the concrete monarchy in favor of theocracy, the direct kingship of God. It is not as though restorative monarchism and theocracy were irreconcilable. The idea of theocracy also plays an important role in documents embodying restorative monarchism. The following distinction is therefore more appropriate: theocracy together *with* restorative monarchism versus pure theocracy *with-*

---

1. For example, Werner H. Schmidt, "Die Ohnmacht des Messias," *KuD* 15 (1969): 18–34, merely notes the increasing passivity of messianism without inquiring into it.

48

out an actual monarchy. For simplicity's sake we shall call the latter the theocratic movement. We are using the term "theocracy" (which goes back to Flavius Josephus) in a somewhat different sense from its usual meaning in recent scholarship,[2] where it refers to the static dominion of God, satisfied with the present, in contrast to the dynamic eschatological school looking to the future. In our terminology, eschatological texts can easily be theocratic. Otherwise, the objective observations on which the other terminology is based are worth heeding. It will be seen that elimination of the concrete monarchy often goes hand in hand with a lack of interest in a future realization of salvation, especially of a political nature. But it is quite proper to ask whether there was a real renunciation of eschatological salvation, even in the writings that appear to be satisfied with the present.[3] We shall ignore this controversy and make a clear distinction between restorative monarchism on the one hand and renunciation of the concrete monarchy on the other. At the moment, we are concerned only to describe the two movements in rough outline. A more precise historical and literary analysis is reserved for Chapters 8–10 and 11–12 (and 13), below.

Restorative monarchism had a basis in fact, since the Davidic family continued to exist,[4] albeit in political impotence. Those involved were probably the descendants of King Jehoiachin, who had been deported to Babylon in 597 B.C. and pardoned by Amel-Marduk in 560 B.C. The Persians even appointed Zerubbabel, a grandson of Jehoiachin, as governor. The Judahite prince Sheshbazzar, mentioned in Ezra 1:8, 11; 5:14, 16, whom the Persians

---

2. See Otto Plöger, *Theocracy and Eschatology*, trans. S. Rudman (Oxford: Blackwell, 1968); Odil H. Steck, "Das Problem theologischer Strömungen in nachexilischer Zeit," *EvTh* 28 (1968): 445–58; Wilhelm T. In der Smitten, *Gottesherrschaft und Gemeinde*, EHS.T 42 (Bern: Lang, 1974).

3. Rudolf Mosis, *Untersuchungen zur Theologie des chronistischen Geschichtswerkes*, FThSt 92 (Freiburg: Herder, 1973), ascribes a future-oriented hope for salvation to the Chronicler, whom he rightly characterizes as having no messianic expectations.

4. See Zech. 12:7, 8, 10, 12; Ezra 8:2; 1 Chron. 3:17–18. The doubts expressed by Diether Lauenstein, *Der Messias* (Stuttgart: Urachhaus, 1971), concerning the continuity of the royal Davidic line can be ignored.

put in charge of repatriation, may be identical with the Shenazzar mentioned in 1 Chron. 3:18, who was a son of Jehoiachin.

What must be objected to is the almost universal equation of restorative monarchism with messianism. There is no evidence for true messianism until the second century B.C.[5] What we are dealing with in the interim is the restoration of preexilic institutions, as a glance at priesthood and prophecy will show.

With the end of the monarchy, the priesthood took on increased importance, especially the office of high priest. In the future the king had to tolerate the existence of the high priest as a rival. This dyarchy of king and priest can already be observed in Zechariah 3, 4, and 6.[6] In the Book of Ezekiel (40–48), the priesthood even predominates. Later this dyarchy, translated into messianic terms, was to be characteristic of the Qumran community, which followed priestly traditions; there the priestly messiah was preeminent. For now, however, we are concerned with the early postexilic period. The priesthood was very soon to outdistance the monarchy, for whereas restorative monarchism, which never amounted to more than a hope, quickly collapsed under the pressure of reality, the priesthood never ceased to function. Religiously speaking, it was never felt to be a rival of Yahweh, and in the eyes of whatever great power was in control it was politically innocuous.

The very observation that hopes and expectations adapt promptly to the situation is instructive. Above all, however, we may gather that the substance of these hopes was not a form of messianism but the restoration of earlier institutions, including the monarchy if at all possible. Therefore, in the Deuteronomistic restoration program in Deut. 17:14—18:22 and in Jer. 33:14–26, the monarch, the priest, and the prophets (or the monarch and the priests) share the same status as institutions. It is inappropriate to ascribe a special messianic status to the kingship.

The prophets became involved in the catastrophe of 586 B.C. because they had been closely associated with the monarchy be-

---

5. See below, Chapter 14.
6. I have been unable to examine Sountilon M. Siahaan, *Die Konkretisierung der Messiasvorstellung nach dem Zusammenbruch Jerusalems* (Hamburg: Schultze, 1973).

fore the exile; as a professional class, they functioned, so to speak, as political guarantors of the relationship between God and the monarchy. The period without kings is therefore necessarily a period without prophets.[7] Zechariah 13:2–6 is even a polemic against prophecy, written by an author whose theocratic position also leads him to ignore the kingship.[8] Elsewhere prophecy is transferred theocratically to the entire nation (Joel 3:1–3 [Eng. 2:28–30]; Isa. 61:1ff.), after analogy with the transfer of kingship.[9] In Deut. 18:15–22, however, prophecy appears alongside kingship and priesthood as an object of the Deuteronomist's restorative hopes. At the time of Zerubbabel (520 B.C.), who it was hoped would restore the monarchy, prophecy raised its head once more in Haggai and Zechariah. In late Judaism it was to be projected into the future eschaton, a development already signaled in Mal. 3:1, 23 (where nothing is said about the monarchy). Then the eschatological prophet has his place alongside the priestly messiah and the princely messiah.[10]

The literary deposit of restorative monarchism—the Deuteronomistic History and the books of Jeremiah, Ezekiel, Hosea, and Amos, as well as Haggai and Zechariah 1–8—is out of proportion to its historical importance. More significant was the purely theocratic movement. Its extent is not yet fully recognized by scholarship because certain exegetical positions stand in the way. A fragmentary grasp of the situation occasionally leads to smoke-screen tactics and talk of "messianism without a messiah." This word game is meant to give the impression of an ongoing messianic expectation but should be avoided in the interests of a clear presentation of history.

Typical features accompanying the theocratic movement are emphasis on the kingship of Yahweh, transfer of the earthly mon-

---

7. See Ps. 74:9; Lam. 2:9; Dan. 3:38. The "extinction of prophecy" after Ezra was later to be a theme of Jewish theology; see Thomas Willi, "Das Erlöschen des Geistes," *Jud.* 28 (1972): 110–16.

8. See below, Chapter 11.

9. See below, Chapter 11.

10. See IQS ix. 11; 4QFlor; John 1:21, 25; 6:14; 7:40; also 1 Macc. 4:46; 9:27; 14:41 (earlier). For the most recent discussion of "prophetic messianism," which we shall not pursue any further, see Joseph Coppens, *Le messianisme et sa relève prophétique*, BEThL 38 (Gembloux: Duculot, 1974); also the review by L. Sabourin in *Bib.* 57 (1976): 140–42.

archy to foreign rulers, and the collectivizing transfer of kingship to the nation as a whole. This last aspect will be discussed separately in Chapter 11, below.

The idea of Yahweh's kingship appears with striking frequency in exilic and postexilic texts, where it is in fact found almost exclusively.[11] That the idea itself is of preexilic and ultimately Canaanite origin[12] can be considered certain but does not alter the evidence under consideration here. Outstanding but by no means isolated witnesses are the psalms of Yahweh's kingship (Psalms 47; 93; 96–99). Deutero-Isaiah's proclamation of the kingship of Yahweh in Isa. 52:7–12 has no chronological or literary priority. All in all, we are dealing with widely dispersed evidence of a single theocratic movement. It is impossible to resist the impression that Yahweh is introduced as king of Israel in a way that leaves no room for an earthly monarchy, of which there is in fact no mention.[13] To the extent that the monarchy is not transferred ideally to the nation as a whole, it is replaced by the direct kingship of Yahweh. This development is not merely the consequence of political realities; the hope for salvation was so lofty by itself that it could do without the earthly institution.

Lack of interest in the concrete monarchy leads occasionally to another highly instructive concomitant of theocratic thought, namely, the transfer of earthly power to foreign rulers. A com-

---

11. See Exod. 15:18; Isa. 24:23; 33:17, 22; 41:21; 43:15; 44:6; 52:7–12; Jer. 10:7, 10; 46:18; 48:15; 51:57; Ezek. 20:33; Obad. 21; Mic. 2:12–13; 4:6–7; Zeph. 3:14–15; Zech. 14:9ff., 16–17; Mal. 1:14; Ps. 10:16; 22:29 (Eng. v. 28); 24:7, 9, 10; 29:10; 47: 48:3 (Eng. v. 2); 68:25 (Eng. v. 24); 84:4, 10 (Eng. vv. 3, 9); 93; 95:3; 96–99; 145:1; 146:10; 149:2; 1 Chron. 29:11. Other passages that may be exilic or postexilic include Ps. 5:3 (Eng. v. 2); 44:5 (Eng. v. 4); 74:12. It is impossible to make a complete list because there are implicit passages like Isa. 40:3ff., 9ff.; 42:13–16; 49:10; Ps. 46:5 (Eng. v. 4); 48:2, 9, 15 (Eng. vv. 1, 8, 14); 69:35 (Eng. v. 34) (see Becker, *Psalmen*, pp. 47–48, and *Wege*, p. 94); 76:3, 12 (Eng. vv. 2, 11); 100; 102:13 (Eng. v. 12); 103:19.

12. See Schmidt, *Königtum Gottes*.

13. See Becker, *Isaias*, pp. 42–43. The situation is summarized by Otto Eissfeldt, "Jahwe als König," *ZAW* 46 (1928): 81–105, reprinted in his *Kleine Schriften* (Tübingen: Mohr, 1962–), 1:171–93, esp. 179–81; Kraus, *Königsherrschaft*, esp. pp. 109–12; Joseph Coppens, "La relève du messianisme royale," *EThL* 47 (1971): 117–43, with comprehensive bibliography.

promising situation for the traditional picture of messianic expectation! As early as Jer. 25:9; 27:6; and 43:10 (probably formulated after the time of Jeremiah), Nebuchadnezzar is called the servant of Yahweh;[14] Isaiah 44:28 and 45:1 hail the Persian Cyrus as the "shepherd" and the "anointed" of Yahweh. This is in line with the position of Cyrus in the Chronicler's history, where the edict of Cyrus (2 Chron. 36:22–23; Ezra 1:1–4) claims that all earthly power has been given to him. The royal throne of Yahweh, which, in the Chronicler's view, was once occupied by David and Solomon,[15] has been transferred to Cyrus.[16] Postexilic Judaism did not hesitate to pray for the Babylonian (Jer. 29:7; Bar. 1:11), Persian (Ezra 6:10), and Seleucid (1 Macc. 7:33) sovereigns, who in turn as heirs of the kings of Judah took over support of the sanctuary (Ezra 1; 6:4, 8ff.; 7:15; Neh. 11:23; 2 Macc. 3:3).[17] This attitude is found even in late Judaism. Flavius Josephus, who thinks in theocratic terms, predicted on the basis of messianic prophecies that the Flavian house would gain sovereignty. In the second century c.e. there is evidence from rabbinic literature that the Jews turned to the Parthian empire, which was hostile to Rome.[18]

---

14. Ezek. 21:32 also probably refers to Nebuchadnezzar; see William L. Moran, "Gen. 49,10 and Its Use in Ez. 21,32," *Bib.* 39 (1958): 405–25; Walther Zimmerli, *Ezekiel,* Hermeneia (Philadelphia: Fortress, 1979), ad loc.; Rafael Criado, "Mesianismo en Ezequiel 21,32," in 30th Semana Bíblica Española, 1970, *La esperanza en la Biblia* (Madrid, 1972), pp. 263–317.

15. See 1 Chron. 17:14; 28:5; 29:23; 2 Chron. 9:8.

16. See Klaus Baltzer, "Das Ende des Staates Juda und die Messias-Frage," in *Studien zur Theologie der alttestamentlichen Überlieferungen,* Festschrift G. von Rad, ed. R. Rendtorff and K. Koch (Neukirchen: Verlag des Erziehungsvereins, 1961), pp. 33–43, esp. pp. 39–40. Baltzer's analysis is challenged by Mosis, *Untersuchungen,* pp. 211–14; it is indisputable, however, that the earthly power is in the hands of Cyrus.

17. R. Pautrel, "Le style de cour et psaume LXXII," in *À la rencontre de Dieu: Mémorial A. Gelin,* BFCTL 8 (Le Puy: Mappus, 1961), pp. 157–63, interprets Psalm 72 as a prayer for the Persian king. Couroyer, "Dieu ou Roi," takes Psalm 45 as referring originally to a Ptolemaic ruler. For our interpretation, see below, Chapter 11.

18. See Kurt Schubert, "Die Entwicklung der eschatologischen Naherwartung im Frühjudentum," in *Vom Messias zum Christus,* ed. K. Schubert (Vienna: Herder, 1964), pp. 1–54, esp. p. 13.

8

The Restorative Monarchism
of the Deuteronomistic History

Only redaction criticism can demonstrate that a restorative monarchism is expressed in the Deuteronomistic History. It was once again Martin Noth[1] who brought to the attention of scholars the fact that the editorial work on the sources bore the stamp of a uniform conception. What we are really concerned with is the purpose expressed by the Deuteronomist throughout the entire work. We are even of the opinion that the sources of the work are even more Deuteronomistic than Noth and the scholars who follow him admit.[2] These sources, too, may be included in our study.

Noth found the kerygma of the Deuteronomist in a retrospective justification for the judgment upon Israel which culminated in the destruction of Jerusalem. This negative perspective is unlikely, if only because in the period when the work was given its final form, which must be after 560 B.C., we find imminent hope for salvation everywhere. This hope also appears—with the reserve expected of a historian—in the kerygma of the Deuteronomist,[3] in part in the form of a restorative monarchism.[4] Of course

---

1. *Überlieferungsgeschichtliche Studien*, 2d ed. (Darstadt: Wissenschaftliche Buchgesellschaft, 1957).

2. See R. A. Carlson, *David, the Chosen King* (Stockholm: Almqvist, 1964). This view is also supported to some extent by Timo Veijola, *Die ewige Dynastie*, AASF 193 (Helsinki: Suomalainen Tiedeakatemia, 1975).

3. This was pointed out by Hans Walter Wolff, "Das Kerygma des deuteronomistischen Geschichtswerkes," ZAW 73 (1961): 171–86, reprinted in his *Gesammelte Studien zum Alten Testament*, TB 22, 2d ed. (Munich: Kaiser, 1973), pp. 308–24; Wolff, however, ignores the monarchism.

4. See Gerhard von Rad, "The Deuteronomic Theology of History in *I*

this single aspect does not exhaust the concerns and themes of the work. Also pursued systematically are the covenant with Yahweh, the Jerusalem temple, the office of prophet and the power of the prophetic word to shape history, and the priesthood of the Zadokites. The monarchy is a central feature, even in Deut. 17:14–20 and 28:36, where it is discussed with the restraint appropriate to a speech placed in the mouth of Moses. The supposed difference between the picture of the king in Deuteronomy and that found in the other portions of the Deuteronomistic History is purely fictional.[5] Despite the antimonarchical skirmishing, which is purely tactical, the monarchy is fundamentally affirmed and deliberately pursued to its goal. The author arrives quickly at the Davidic monarchy, which he hopes to see restored. David is the ideal king.[6] Even the narratives of David's rise allude to his being Yahweh's elect.[7]

In the structure of the work, the prophecy of Nathan in 2 Samuel 7 occupies a key position.[8] In its present form, it is an interpretation given by the Deuteronomist, relevant to his own age; he sets it in a place of supreme importance in the interests of his monarchism.[9] Nathan prophesies that the Davidic dynasty will endure forever even in case of failure; on this promise the Deuteronomist rests his hopes.

and *II Kings*," in his *Problem of the Hexateuch*, pp. 205–21; idem, *Old Testament Theology*, trans. D. M. G. Stalker (Edinburgh: Oliver, 1962), 1:334–47; Baltzer, "Ende," pp. 37–39; Carlson, *David*; Walter Brueggemann, "Isaiah 55 and Deuteronomic Theology," *ZAW* 80 (1968): 191–203; Erich Zenger, "Die deuteronomistische Interpretation der Rehabilitierung Johachins," *BZ*, n.f., 12 (1968): 16–30; Kellermann, *Messias*, pp. 81–83. Roderick A. F. MacKenzie, "The Messianism of DT," *CBQ* 19 (1957): 299–305, and Rolf Knierim, "Die Messianologie des ersten Buches Samuel," *EvTh* 30 (1970): 113–33, have nothing to contribute to our question.

5. Contrary to Poulssen, *König und Tempel*, pp. 108–9, 120, 127; see my review in *Bib.* 50 (1969): 423.

6. See 1 Kings 3:3; 9:4; 11:4, 6, 13, 32ff., 38; 14:8; 15:3, 5, 11; 2 Kings 14:3; 16:2; 18:3; 22:2.

7. See 1 Sam. 13:13–14; 25:28, 30; 2 Sam. 3:9, 18; 5:2.

8. See Dennis J. McCarthy, "II Samuel 7 and the Structure of the Deuteronomic History," *JBL* 84 (1965): 131–38; McCarthy does not, however, discuss the work's monarchism.

9. See our earlier discussion, above, in Chapter 4.

Among other evidence, the prophecy of Nathan betrays its Deuteronomistic position through the recapitulation of history in 2 Sam. 7:11, 15. In addition, it solves a problem that must have bothered the later period: Why was it not David, the ideal king, but Solomon, who built the temple? Yahweh's instructions explain this fact, which could never be hidden.[10] The Deuteronomist gives his commentary on the prophecy of Nathan in the prayer of David that follows (2 Sam. 7:19–29) and gives voice to his hope especially in verses 19, 25, and 28–29.

In the subsequent course of his presentation, he never loses sight of the central issue of the prophecy of Nathan. For him prophetic predictions are to be taken seriously, and he conscientiously records their fulfillment.[11] No prophetic word "falls down."[12] The following passages illustrate how the prophecy of Nathan functions: 1 Kings 1:48; 2:4, 24, 33, 45; 5:19 (Eng. v. 5); 8:24ff.; 9:5; 11:11ff., 34, 36, 39; 13:2; 15:4; 2 Kings 3:14; 8:19; 2 Kings 11 (the dynasty in danger); 19:34; 20:5; 20:8 (prediction of the captivity of Jehoiachin and his sons); 21:7ff. To the extent that the passages derive from sources, they have been employed by the Deuteronomist to serve his monarchic hopes. But it is worth reconsidering the question of whether the passages themselves are not Deuteronomistic, or whether perhaps the sources themselves have a similar concern. The series ends with the eloquent conclusion of the work in 2 Kings 25:27–30: the freeing of Jehoiachin in the year 560 B.C. is taken as a sign of hope.[13] The Deuteronomist obviously attaches great importance

---

10. Besides 2 Samuel 7, see also 1 Kings 8:18–19. In 1 Kings 5:17 another explanation is made available: Because of his many wars, David had no time. For the Chronicler, the problem was even more pressing. He has David make preparations for construction and explains David's failure to build the temple as being due to his being a man of war and having shed so much blood (see 1 Chron. 22:8; 28:3).

11. See especially Von Rad, "Deuteronomic Theology." Note the following correspondences: Josh. 6:26 / 1 Kings 16:34; 2 Sam. 7:13 / 1 Kings 8:15–21, 24–26; 1 Kings 11:29ff. / 12:15; 1 Kings 13 / 2 Kings 23:16–18; 1 Kings 14:6ff. / 15:29; 1 Kings 16:1ff. / 16:12; 1 Kings 21:19–24 / 22:38 (following the delay of 21:27–29) as well as 2 Kings 9:25–26, 36–37 together with 10:10–11; 1 Kings 22:17 / 22:35–36; 2 Kings 1:4, 6, 16 / 1:17; 2 Kings 21:10–15 / 24:2; 22:15–20 / 23:30 and 2 Kings 24–25.

12. For this idiom see Josh. 21:45; 23:14; 1 Kings 8:56; 2 Kings 10:10.

13. See Zenger, "Rehabilitierung."

to Jehoiachin and his offspring, thereby reaching a decision in the question of legitimacy that had been raised in 597 B.C., when Zedekiah became king instead of his nephew Jehoiachin.[14]

A picture of the monarchy as imagined by the Deuteronomist is painted in Deut. 17:14–20. The ruler is subjected to Yahwistic discipline; the allures of the royal ideology are not tolerated. This alone is enough to make the statement about sonship in 2 Sam. 7:14 different from Ps. 2:7; 110:3(?); and Isa. 9:5 (Eng. v. 6), which reflect the royal ideology.[15]

In 1 Chronicles 17 and the poetic restatements in Psalms 89 and 132, the prophecy of Nathan did not retain its function of giving voice to restorative monarchism.[16]

---

14. On the question of legitimacy, see Martin Noth, "Die Katastrophe von Jerusalem im Jahre 587 v. Chr. und ihre Bedeutung für Israel," in his *Gesammelte Studien,* pp. 346–71; Baltzer, "Ende," p. 36; Zimmerli, *Ezekiel,* pp. 114–15.

15. See above, Chapter 4, note 8.

16. See above, Chapters 12 and 11, respectively.

9

Restorative Monarchism in the Prophetic Books

What the Deuteronomist introduces into his historical account is present in certain prophetic books (Jeremiah, Ezekiel, Hosea, Amos) in the form of a redactionally contrived prophetic prediction. As in the case of the Deuteronomist, we find ourselves in the domain of exilic and postexilic preaching of salvation. Characteristically, the books just mentioned (except for Ezekiel) have undergone Deuteronomistic redaction. Within the context of the same message of salvation, they stand in contrast to the theocratic books of Isaiah and Micah, as well as Zechariah 9–14.[1] Zechariah 1–8 and Haggai will be examined separately in the next chapter. The other prophetic books are of interest only in that their silence bears witness to the messianic vacuum.

For an evaluation of the passages from the Book of Jeremiah, it is essential to distinguish the words of the prophet himself from the statements of the book. Unfortunately there is no generally accepted position from which we can start. A certain authority attaches to a division into genuine words of Jeremiah, a so-called Baruch narrative, and words of Jeremiah that have been Deuteronomistically edited.[2] There is much to suggest that the oracles of religious optimism belong to the Deuteronomistic sections, which may derive from the redactor of the book.[3]

The historical Jeremiah polemicized against the contemporary

---

1. See below, Chapter 11.
2. This division was proposed by Mowinckel, who is followed today by Wilhelm Rudolph, *Jeremia*, HAT, ser. 1, vol. 12, 3d ed. (Tübingen: Mohr, 1968).
3. The most recent discussion of the redactional problems is furnished

kings.[4] In view of his devastating oracle against Jehoiachin (Jer. 22:24–30), he probably decided in Zedekiah's favor in the question of legitimacy.[5] He gave a real chance to Zedekiah, who reigned from 597 to 586 B.C. This would be in agreement with the theory that 23:5–6, now wholly framed and swallowed up by redactional passages, could originally have been a genuine designation oracle of Jeremiah in favor of Zedekiah. The former Mattaniah in fact received from Nebuchadnezzar the name Zedekiah (see 2 Kings 24:17), echoes of which are heard in 23:6 in the name *yahweh ṣidqēnû*, "Yahweh is our righteousness." It should likewise be noted that the redactional passage 33:15–16 borrows and changes the textual form of 23:5–6, apparently applying the name *yahweh ṣidqēnû* to Judah and Jerusalem. This circumstance might suggest that 23:5–6 was available to the redactor in his sources.

After the fall of Zedekiah, his blinding, and the execution of his sons, the chapter of the Davidic monarchy was closed for Jeremiah. Nothing in the convictions of the time necessitated a future for the house of David, not to speak of a Davidic messiah. After the end of the Davidic monarchy, Jeremiah seems to have rested his modest politico-religious hopes in Gedaliah, the governor appointed by Nebuchadnezzar, who had his residence in Mizpah. Gedaliah was not of Davidic descent.[6] In 2 Kings 25:22–26, the Deuteronomist assigns no importance to Gedaliah; in chapter 52, which largely incorporates 2 Kings 25, the *Book* of Jeremiah even omits the passage about Gedaliah. Both hope that the family of Jehoiachin will regain the kingship. The account in

---

by Helga Weippert, *Die Prosareden des Jeremiabuches*, BZAW 132 (Berlin: de Gruyter, 1973). With respect to the increasingly accepted theory of Deuteronomistic redaction, this work is backward-looking. The following studies dealing specifically with the optimistic texts appear to point the way: Herrmann, *Heilserwartungen*, pp. 155–241; Kellermann, *Messias*, pp. 33–36, 78–80 (although he considers Jer. 23:5–6 genuine). The traditional approach is represented by Angelo Penna, "Il messianismo nel libro di Geremia," in *Messianismo*, pp. 35–56. Seybold, *Königtum*, pp. 115–32 fails to state the problems of literary and redaction criticism sharply enough.

4. See Jer. 13:13–14, 18; 21:11–14; 22:10–19, 24–30; 29:16.
5. See also 28:4 and the position of the prophet expressed there. On the question of legitimacy, see above, Chapter 8, note 14.
6. See especially Baltzer, "Ende," pp. 33–37.

Jeremiah 39ff. takes a different approach and probably represents the attitude of the historical Jeremiah. In 40:11–12, a full-scale return of the diaspora to Gedaliah is signalized, together with removal of the curse through the blessing of a good harvest. According to 41:10, the royal princesses had been entrusted to Gedaliah, a statement that may allude discretely to his quasi-royal position.[7] The murder of Gedaliah—by a descendant of David!—is branded a crime. Later, too, the Gedaliah episode seems to have been considered important; for even in the year 518 B.C. a fast was held in the seventh month commemorating the murder of Gedaliah (see Zech. 7:5; 8:19). After Gedaliah's end, Jeremiah, who had been transported to Egypt, buried his final hopes for the monarchy.

Not so the (Deuteronomistic) redaction of the *Book* of Jeremiah. To this redaction we may assign the optimistic texts concerning the monarchy, while there is no place for them in the preaching of the historical Jeremiah. But the monarchy is far from being the focus of the message of religious optimism; so important a text as Jer. 31:31–34 can dispense with it. The chief witness to the hopes of monarchism is the passage 23:5–6. As a redactional proclamation of religious optimism, it is clearly set apart from the preceding threats of Jeremiah against the royal house and is surrounded by passages bearing a Deuteronomistic stamp (23:1–4, 7–8). The redaction of the book, like the Deuteronomistic History, probably had in mind the descendants of Jehoiachin. The resulting position with respect to the question of legitimacy may be expressed in the phrase *ṣemaḥ ṣaddîq*, which can mean not only "righteous branch" but also "legitimate branch."[8] With 23:5–6 belong 3:15; 22:2, 4; 30:9, 21; and 33:14–26. The last passage, which is not in the Septuagint but is typically Deuteronomistic, places the monarchy as an institution alongside the priesthood. There is no justification for making qualitative distinctions, as though in 33:14–26 we were dealing

---

7. Compare 2 Sam. 12:8ff., the actions of Absalom in 2 Sam. 16:21–22, and Solomon's reaction to the demands of Adonijah in 1 Kings 2:13–25. The action of Reuben in Gen. 35:22 (compare 49:4) may be based on an attempted usurpation (in tribal history?).

8. See James Swetnam, "Some Observations on the Background of *sdyq* in Jeremias 23,5a," *Bib.* 46 (1965): 29–40.

with restorative monarchism but elsewhere with true messianism. The Book of Jeremiah closes (not by chance) with the statement about the rehabilitation of Jehoiachin (52:31–34) taken from 2 Kings 25:27–30. The passage 31:22, traditionally influential, has no bearing on the subject.[9]

While it is possible, albeit difficult, to distinguish the words of the prophet from the redactional sections in the Book of Jeremiah, all attempts to draw a profile of the historical Ezekiel fail. With some confidence we may find polemic against the monarchy in 12:10ff. (against Zedekiah), 17:1–21 (Jehoiachin and Zedekiah), 21:30–32 (Eng. vv. 25–27) (Zedekiah; see v. 28 [Eng. v. 23]), and 7:27; 22:6, 25, as well as a lament for the royal house in 19:1–14, where only 19:2–4 refers with certainty to Jehoahaz, the rest referring either to Zedekiah or to Jehoiachin or to Jehoiakim (vv. 5–9) and Jehoiachin (vv. 10–14). It can also be asked whether the historical Ezekiel—unlike Jeremiah—did not cherish a continuing hope with reference to the royal house of David. Since the polemical passages rule out Zedekiah, Jehoiachin and his descendants would once again be involved. Noth[10] interprets 19:10–14 as a decision, albeit only provisional, in favor of Jehoiachin, but other authors find in the passage a reference to Zedekiah or Jehoiakim. Fohrer[11] finds in 21:32 the hope expressed for a reappointment of Jehoiachin, but the passage actually refers to Nebuchadnezzar.[12] Zimmerli[13] considers 17:22–24 an optimistic oracle concerning Jehoiachin, deriving from the historical Ezekiel; but it remains doubtful whether a royal figure is meant here at all (see the further discussion below). For a favorable view of Jehoiachin on the part of Ezekiel, the following observations might also come into play. As one of those carried off in 597 B.C., the prophet shared the king's fate, as it were; 11:14–21 and 33:23–29 bear witness to a kind of animosity toward those left

---

9. See Claus Schedl, " 'Femina circumdabit virum' oder 'via salutis,' " *ZKTh* 83 (1961): 431–42; William L. Holladay, "Jer XXXI 22B Reconsidered: 'The Woman Encompasses the Man,' " *VT* 16 (1966): 236–39.

10. "Katastrophe," pp. 361–67.

11. Georg Fohrer, *Ezechiel*, HAT, ser. 1, vol. 13 (Tübingen: Mohr, 1955), ad loc.

12. See the literature cited above, Chapter 7, note 14.

13. *Ezekiel*, ad loc.

behind. With the exception of 24:1-2, the book always dates events from the captivity of Jehoiachin, explicitly so in 1:2 and 40:1.

But the attempt to determine the attitude of the historical Ezekiel founders on the problem of the figure himself. The preaching of Ezekiel has passed through the forge of tradition and has been absorbed by the theology of the book,[14] even if those scholars who consider the book pseudepigraphic are wrong.[15]

Undoubtedly, the Book of Ezekiel enshrines a monarchic expectation, but it must not be understood in a messianic sense.[16] The passages involved are: 34:23-24; 37:22, 24-25; 43:7ff.; 44:3; 45:7-8, 16-17, 22; 46:2, 4, 8, 10, 12-13, 16-17; 48:21-22. It is doubtful whether 29:21 refers to the kingship. Probably 17:22-24 is also a theocratic oracle of favor, to be interpreted as referring to the nation.[17] One should have no illusions about the status accorded the king in the book's expectations: He stands in the shadow of theocracy and the privileged priesthood. His saving function is hardly recognizable. In 34:23-24 and 37:22, 24-25 he appears as guarantor of the nation's unity, but Yahweh himself is the actual shepherd of his people, and he is given the title of king in 20:33. In Ezekiel 43-46 and 48, the king is a supernumerary of the hierocracy, subject to detailed regulation. He is mentioned without any messianic splendor, more for the sake of completeness. The fuller preexilic functions of the kingship are thoroughly dismantled. *Several* princes are mentioned in 45:8-9, and according to 46:16-18 the prince has sons and heirs. The monarchy is thus conceived in dynastic terms; despite the fantasy of the program in Ezekiel 40-48, it keeps its feet solidly on the

---

14. Herrmann, *Heilserwartungen*, pp. 241-91.

15. See, for example, the citations in Jörg Garscha, *Studien zum Ezechielbuch*, EHS.T 23 (Bern: Lang, 1974), pp. 10-11.

16. See W. Gronkowski, *Le messianisme d'Ezéchiel* (Paris: Geuthner, 1930) (not examined); André Caquot, "Le messianisme d'Ezéchiel," *Sem.* 14 (1964): 3-23; Herrmann, *Heilserwartungen*, pp. 241-91; Poulssen, *König*, pp. 146-50; Walther Zimmerli, *Ezechiel*, BK 13/2 (Neukirchen: Neukirchener Verlag, 1969), vol. 2, pp. 915-18; Kellermann, *Messias*, pp. 40-42, 84-89, 107-8; Seybold, *Königtum*, pp. 132-52.

17. Herrmann, *Heilserwartungen*, pp. 258-59, 277.

ground. With respect to the title, the author obviously has reservations. Only in 37:22, 24 do we find the term *melek*, "king," which recalls kingship of the Canaanite type. Else the archaic title *nāśî*, "prince," is used, which has an antimonarchic coloration.[18] The expression "my servant David" in 34:23–24 must not tempt us to the gross misinterpretation of seeing here a David *redivivus*.[19] The context admits no doubt that nothing more is meant than a renewal of the Davidic monarchy. A distinction between the supposedly messianic royal figure in 34:23–24 and 37:22, 24–25 and the vestigial prince in chapters 44–46 and 48 cannot be maintained. The differences in presentation are determined by context. The hypothesis that Ezekiel 40–48 is literarily distinct from Ezekiel 1–39 is not correct.

The dating of the monarchism in the Book of Ezekiel must remain hypothetical. The book could have come into being in the fifth century B.C.

The Book of Amos and the Book of Hosea, too, both of which have undergone Deuteronomistic redaction,[20] record a restorative monarchism. The fallen booth of David in Amos 9:11 that is to be raised up is the Davidic royal house. In the case of Hos. 3:5, it is necessary once again to caution against the mistake of finding a David *redivivus* in the strict sense. Neither of the passages comes from the prophet in question.

---

18. Ephraim A. Speiser, "Background and Function of the Biblical Nāśî'," *CBQ* 25 (1963): 111–17, reprinted in his *Oriental and Biblical Studies,* ed. J. J. Finkelstein and M. Greenberg (Philadelphia: University of Pennsylvania Press, 1967), pp. 113–22, disputes Noth's view that in ancient Israel the *nāśî'* was the spokesman for his tribe at the central sanctuary. Noth's explanation is in fact hypothetical.

19. The same is true in Jer. 30:9 and Hos. 3:5.

20. See Werner H. Schmidt, "Die deuteronomische Redaktion des Amosbuches," *ZAW* 77 (1965): 168–93 (does not include Amos 9:11–12 in the Deuteronomistic redaction, which affects the rest of the book); Hans Walter Wolff, *Joel and Amos,* trans. W. Janzen et al., Hermeneia (Philadelphia: Fortress, 1977), pp. 351–55 (posits a Deuteronomistic redactional stratum in the development of the book, to which, however, Amos 9:11–12 does not belong); Ulrich Kellermann, "Der Amosschluss als Stimme deuteronomistischer Heilshoffnung," *EvTh* 29 (1969): 169–83; idem, *Messias,* p. 38. Determination of the extent of the Deuteronomistic redaction in the Book of Hosea is an unfinished task for scholarship.

10

Zerubbabel

Up to this point we have encountered restorative monarchism only in its literary dress. The Zerubbabel episode, recorded in the Book of Haggai and the Book of Zechariah, provides a model example.[1] We know the date and the cast of characters. The course of events proves once again that there can be no talk of messianism in the strict sense. As tradition would lead us to expect, the hopes associated with Zerubbabel are connected with the rebuilding of the temple and a resurgence of prophecy. Since time immemorial the prophets had been responsible for designating the king. King, temple, and prophet also appear together in the prophecy of Nathan.

In Haggai's designation oracle, Hag. 2:20-23, in which the expressions "my servant" and "chosen" appear, the prophet retracts the threat in Jer. 22:24, which Jeremiah had hurled against Jehoiachin, the grandfather of Zerubbabel. His monarchism has revolutionary overtones; he has in mind events like the dynastic

---

1. Some recent discussions: Robert T. Siebeneck, "The Messianism of Aggeus and Proto-Zacharias," *CBQ* 19 (1957): 312–38; Albert Petitjean, "La mission de Zorobabel et la réconstruction du temple," *EThL* 42 (1966): 40–71; Giovanni Rinaldi, "Il 'germoglio' messianico in Zaccaria 3,8; 6,12," in *Il Messianismo*, pp. 179–91; Willem A. M. Beuken, *Haggai-Sacharja 1–8*, SSN 10 (Assen: Van Gorcum, 1967); Georg Sauer, "Serubbabel in der Sicht Haggais und Sacharjas," in *Das ferne und nahe Wort*, Festschrift L. Rost, ed. F. Maass, BZAW 105 (Berlin: Töpelmann, 1967), pp. 199–207; Werner Dommershausen, "Der 'Spross' als Messias-Vorstellung bei Jeremia und Sacharja," *TThQ* 148 (1968): 321–41; Kellermann, *Messias*, pp. 44–46, 58–62; Karl-Martin Beyse, *Serubbabel und die Königserwartungen der Propheten Haggai und Sacharja*, AzT, ser. 1, 48 (Stuttgart: Calwer, 1972); Klaus Seybold, "Die Königserwartung bei den Propheten Haggau und Sachaja," *Jud.* 28 (1972): 69–78; Wilhelm T. In der Smitten, "Historische Probleme zum Kyrosedikt und zum Jerusalemer Tempelbau von 515," *Persica* 6 (1972/74): 167–78.

64

confusion following the death of Cambyses in 522 B.C.,[2] if he does not actually view the confusion itself as a signal that the turning point has come for Israel's salvation. For Zechariah, the watchword is: Not by might, or by power, but by God's spirit (Zech. 4:6). The earth is quietly at rest (1:11). Nevertheless he too proclaimed oracles of designation for Zerubbabel (3:8; 4; 6:9–15). It is inappropriate to interpret 3:8 messianically while limiting 6:9–15 to a restorative monarchism.[3] Typical of Zechariah is the term *tṣemaḥ*, "branch," which probably derives from the royal ideology.[4] The chain of events was probably not as innocuous as the description in the Book of Zechariah, which has been edited in the spirit of the Chronicler.[5] Most scholars think that 6:9–15 has been reinterpreted so as to apply to the nonpolitical priesthood. The crown, which in the present text is to be set on the head of Joshua the high priest, was probably meant for Zerubbabel in the original version, as can be seen from 6:12–13. The figure of Zerubbabel has been fully neutralized by the theocratically minded Chronicler in Ezra 1–6, especially 4–5, so that he is represented as nothing more than a rebuilder of the temple.[6] Zerubbabel's mysterious disappearance from the stage of history gives cause for thought. Was he recalled under a cloud of suspicion? In the fourth year of Darius (see Zech. 7:1) he still appears to be governor, although not mentioned by name. At the time of the visitation by the satrap Tattenai (Ezra 5:3) he was probably no longer in office. The Book of Zechariah and the Chronicler's history probably have good reasons for their silence.

Haggai and Zechariah give the high priest Joshua a place alongside Zerubbabel. Here we have a historical illustration of the juxtaposition of the two institutions attested to in Jer. 33:14–

---

2. See Hag. 2:6–9, 21–22. The messianizing translation of the Vulgate in 2:8 (*desideratus cunctis gentibus*) has influenced the tradition of interpretation.

3. Rehm, *Der königliche Messias*, pp. 303–13.

4. In Zech. 3:8; 6:12. See also Jer. 23:25; 33:15; 2 Sam. 23:25; Ps. 132:17; and Isa. 4:2. In Isa. 4:2, the term refers to the nation collectively; see Becker, *Isaias*, pp. 49–50.

5. Demonstration of chronistic redaction is one of the goals of Beuken, *Haggai-Sacharja*.

6. See Ulrich Kellermann, *Nehemia*, BZAW 102 (Berlin: Töpelmann, 1967), pp. 96–97.

16 and Deut. 17:14—18:8. A certain primacy of the prince, however, cannot be missed. After Joshua has been named along with (but *after*) Zerubbabel in Hag. 1:1, 12, 14; 2:2, 4, he vanishes from sight in the crucial oracle of designation, 2:20–23. In Zechariah, also, the "two anointed" (Zech. 4:14) do not enjoy quite the same status. The "branch" is treated preferentially. Although the high priest has authority over the temple (3:7), we have not yet arrived at the point where the priesthood takes the prince under its wing, as documented in the Book of Ezekiel, and certainly not at the messianic dyarchy of the Dead Sea Scrolls.[7]

Despite the unfavorable political circumstances, restorative monarchism appears to have revived occasionally even later. In 485 B.C., when the Persian Empire was shaken at the accession of Xerxes by rebellion in Egypt and Babylon, it is conceivable that there were efforts to gain independence in the province of Judah. This is at least suggested by the accusation mentioned in Ezra 4:6.[8] The Zerubbabel episode was also occasioned by a change of rulers. But we have no evidence that the Davidic dynasty was involved in 485 B.C. A further accusation in Ezra 4:7–23 is dated in the reign of Artaxerxes I (465–424 B.C.). It contains the statement that the Jews were trying to rebuild the walls of Jerusalem (see especially 4:12). Since Neh. 1:3 obviously refers to the failure of these efforts, we probably find ourselves in the period of Megabyzus's rebellion, somewhere around 448–446 B.C.[9]

More clear are the events surrounding Nehemiah, who was governor of Judah from 445 to 433 B.C. and who returned to Jerusalem shortly after 433.[10] Nehemiah completed the rebuilding of the walls with the Persians' approval. In the face of repeated accusations by the local princes and governors, he vigorously

---

7. On this dyarchy, see Chapter 7, above, and Chapter 14, below.
8. See Kellermann, *Nehemia*, pp. 184–85, n. 45. To the studies by Morgenstern cited there but rejected should now be added Julian Morgenstern, "Further Light from the Book of Isaiah upon the Catastrophe of 485 B.C.," *HUCA* 37 (1966): 1–28.
9. Kellermann, *Nehemia*, pp. 185–86.
10. Ibid., especially pp. 179–91; idem, "Die politische Messiashoffnung zwischen den Testamenten," *PTh* 56 (1967): 362–77, 436–48; idem, *Messias*, pp. 47–48; In der Smitten, *Gottesherrschaft*.

denied that he was planning a rebellion (see Neh. 2:19ff.; 6). But one can read between the lines in Nehemiah 6 that he gave rise to political hopes and prophetic attempts at legitimation (see 6:10-13). The text itself of course claims to know nothing of such events. Because literary analysis of the Book of Nehemiah is so difficult, we must leave unresolved the question whether Nehemiah himself hushed up the situation in writing his memoirs or whether we should think in terms of similar activity on the part of the Chronicler. It is possible that Nehemiah played an innocent role in the political machinations. The theory that nationalistic circles attempted to use Nehemiah for their own purposes gains in credibility if Nehemiah was a descendant of David. Kellermann considers this likely on the basis of a variety of evidence.[11] According to Neh. 2:3, 5, Nehemiah laments before the king that the city in which his fathers' sepulchers are located lies waste. Does he mean the royal sepulchers? In 1:6 he confesses his own sin and that of his family. Does this refer to the royal family? It was the practice of the Persians to appoint members of the royal house to positions of responsibility, as in the case of Zerubbabel and Sheshbazzar. As governor, Nehemiah waived the allowance due him (5:14-19). Did he have income from crown property at his disposal? The most important piece of evidence is the dubious royal designation itself.

The deportations carried out under Artaxerxes III between 350 and 348 B.C. may also suggest nationalistic expectations. They were undertaken in conjunction with a revolt in Phoenicia.[12] Kellermann[13] also interprets Zech. 9:9-10 as an allusion to royalist hopes in the time of Alexander the Great, which was certainly a time of transition and confusion. Quite apart from the dating of Zechariah 9-11 in the period of Alexander, we do not consider Zech. 9:9-10 as a witness to restorative monarchism.[14]

---

11. *Nehemia*, pp. 156–59. I was not able to obtain the article by Wilhelm T. In der Smitten, "Erwägungen zu Nehemias Davidizität," *JSJ* 5 (1975): 41–48, which is said to modify and extend the arguments of Kellermann; see In der Smitten, *Gottesherrschaft*, pp. 31–63.
12. Kellermann, *Nehemia*, pp. 187–88; idem, *Messias*, p. 49.
13. *Messias*, pp. 49–50.
14. See the discussion of the passage in Chapter 11, below.

11

The Theocratic Theory of the Nation

In Chapter 7, above, the kingship of Yahweh and the transfer of earthly power to foreign rulers were mentioned as characteristic aspects of the theocratic movement. Here we shall discuss a third aspect, which has not been accorded sufficient attention by scholars: the collectivizing transfer of the idea of the king to the nation. The Davidic monarchy and its associated promises had become a resource that was not allowed to lie idle outside the circles of restorative monarchism. The Davidic promise was idealized and transferred to the nation as a whole. The notion of Israel as Yahweh's son[1] may have helped the transfer of the royal predicate "son of God" (See Isa. 9:5 [Eng. v. 6]; Ps. 2:7; 110:3).

Like restorative monarchism, the collective transfer of the idea of the king appears in specific books and literary contexts, specifically the Book of Isaiah, the Book of Micah, Zechariah 9–14, and the royal psalms. The treatment of particular cases must be left to other studies that discuss the theme in greater detail.[2]

The most generally recognized example is Isa. 55:3–5.[3] Yahweh makes an everlasting covenant with Israel. When he calls this

---

1. Applied to the nation as a whole in Exod. 4:22; Jer. 3:19; 31:9, 20; Hos. 11:1; Yahweh is described as Israel's father in Deut. 32:6, 18; Jer. 3:4. The whole theme has now been treated by Werner Schlisske, *Gottessöhne und Gottessohn im Alten Testament*, BWANT 97 (Stuttgart: Kohlhammer, 1973); Vitus Huonder, *Israel, Sohn Gottes*, OBO 6 (Freiburg: Universitätsverlag, 1975).

2. Becker, *Isaias*; also an article entitled "Die kollektive Deutung der Königspsalmen," soon to appear in *ThPh*.

3. See Otto Eissfeldt, "The Promises of Grace to David in Isaiah 55:1–5," in *Israel's Prophetic Heritage*, Festschrift J. Muilenburg, ed. B. W. Ander-

68

covenant "my steadfast, sure love for David," he is not using a simile ("*as* I made a covenant with David") but rather transferring the Davidic covenant to the nation. David was formerly a witness (of Yahweh's power) to the peoples; now Israel takes over this role. Israel calls nations it does not know, and nations that did not know Israel run to it. Israel also appears as a witness in Isa. 43:19 and 44:8. Other passages voicing Israel's dominion over the nations include Isa. 45:14; 49:7, 22–23; 60:14. The phraseology of such passages characteristically borrows from the royal psalms (see Ps. 72:9–11); the relationship between Isa. 55:4–5 and Ps. 18:44–45, 48 is quite clear. This gives further support to a transfer of the idea of the king.

Isaiah 55:3–5 must be seen in the total context of Isaiah 40–55. The passage is only the tip of the iceberg. In Isaiah 40–55, the kingship of Yahweh occupies an outstanding place;[4] in good theocratic fashion, earthly power is accorded the Persian Cyrus.[5] The purely ideal transfer of kingship of the people combined with the abandonment of realistic hopes of renewal of the monarchy should therefore come as no surprise. Above all, the servant songs belong in this category.[6] They are to be viewed as belonging to the continuum of Deutero-Isaiah (Isaiah 40–55) and should be interpreted collectively.[7] Israel is the servant of Yah-

---

son (New York: Harper, 1962), pp. 196ff.; Becker, "Kollektive Deutung"; idem, "Jesaja 55:1–3," in *Die alttestamentlichen Lesungen*, A, 2:141–52, esp. 145–48. On earlier studies, some of which err in proposing a messianic interpretation, see Coppens, "Relève," pp. 100ff. The transfer of the idea of the king to the nation has recently been misconstrued by Willem A. M. Beuken, "Isa. 55,3–5," *Bijd.* 35 (1974): 49–64. A basically accurate discussion will be found in Seybold, *Königtum*, pp. 152–62.

4. See 41:21; 43:15; 44:6, and above all the proclamation in 52:7–12, as well as a whole series of passages in which the notion of Yahweh as king is implicit.

5. In 44:28 and 45:1; see above, Chapter 7.

6. Usually defined as Isa. 42:1–9; 49:1–6; 50:4–11; 52:13—53:12.

7. See Becker, *Isaias*, pp. 38–39; more recently idem, "Kollektive Deutung 3," where a brief survey of current and past scholarship is given. Today the scholars who espouse the collective interpretation include Otto Kaiser, *Der königliche Knecht*, FRLANT 70, 2d ed. (Göttingen: Vandenhoeck, 1962), with a summary on pp. 132–34; Norman H. Snaith, "Isaiah 40–66," in *Studies on the Second Part of the Book of Isaiah*, VT.S 14 (Leiden: Brill, 1967), pp. 135–264; Norbert Lohfink, " 'Israel' in Jes 49,3," in *Wort, Lied, und Gottesspruch*, pp. 217–29 (contests the usual deletion of "Israel" in Isa. 49:3); Leland E. Wilshire, "Servant-City," *JBL* 94 (1975): 356–67.

weh; at most the more precise definition of the collective entity is open to debate (the ideal Israel, the sacred remnant, the exilic community, the daughter of Zion). Among other things, the servant of Yahweh has certain royal features, so that here too we may register a transfer of the kingship of the nation.[8] It would lead to an unjustified mystification of the historical picture of messianic expectation if, on the basis of an interpretation that sees the servant of Yahweh as an individual, one were to find a messianic figure without roots in the intellectual and spiritual milieu of the time. The spiritualized picture of the messiah in the exilic period is based on understandable wishful thinking. The traditional assignment of messianic status to certain texts changes unconsciously into critical exegesis.

The redaction of the Book of Isaiah in Isaiah 1–39 also thinks in theocratic terms. The presuppositions necessary for an understanding of the situation are too far-reaching to be developed in detail here. Above all, it is necessary to take into account the reinterpretation of earlier texts in the redaction of the prophetic books.[9] While incorporating the literary remains of the early prophets, the prophetic books pursue their own purposes, from the perspective of preaching salvation in the exilic and postexilic period. In the Book of Isaiah, the classic messianic passages 4:2; 7:14 (and 8:8); 8:23—9:6 (Eng. 9:1–7); and 11:1–5 have undergone theocratizing and collectivizing reinterpretation. In question at 4:2 is the royal predicate *ṣemaḥ*, "branch";[10] at 8:23—9:6 (Eng. 9:1–7) and 11:1–5, Isaianic compositions related to the king's en-

---

8. See, for example, Kaiser, *Der königliche Knecht*. The servant also exhibits features of the petitioner who speaks in the individual psalms of lament, the language of which has influenced Deutero-Isaiah (see Becker, *Wege*, pp. 64–65), and above all prophetic features. Transfer of the prophetic office to the nation also appears in Joel 3:1–3 (Eng. 2:28–30) and Isa. 61:1ff., where the anointing of prophets (see 1 Kings 19:16; Ps. 105:15) is applied to Israel.

9. See Becker, *Isaias*, pp. 33–68; also idem, *Israel*, pp. 10–39, esp. pp. 35–37. The redactio-critical approach to the prophetic books has gained increasing attention in recent years. We may single out for its methodological approach Otto Kaiser, *Isaiah 13–39;* trans. R. A. Wilson, OTL (Philadelphia: Westminster, 1974); see my review of the German original in *ThRv* 70 (1974): 201–5.

10. See above, Chapter 10, note 4.

thronement and bearing the stamp of the royal ideology; and at 7:14, Isaiah's Immanuel oracle.[11] The redaction of the Book of Isaiah sees in the figure of the king, or the figure of Immanuel, the nation of Israel with emphasis on the increase of the nation, a constant concern of the exilic and postexilic community.[12] The basis for the reinterpretation was the motif of "birth" (7:14; 9:5 [Eng. 9:6]) and the "branch" (4:2; 11:11).

Two other royal passages in Isaiah 1–39, which have received little notice, are 16:1, 5 and 32:1. Isaianic authorship is probably not to be considered seriously. Wildberger,[13] who is always hesitant to declare a passage not genuine, cites a wealth of observations with respect to 16:1, 5 that prevent him from putting the text in the same category as the Isaianic royal texts in Isaiah 7–11. Thus we are faced with two alternatives: Either 16:1, 5 (and 32:1) are an expression of exilic or postexilic monarchism, or they were added by the theocratic redaction of the Book of Isaiah. The influence of the redactional reinterpretation must be judged very strong, at least in Isaiah 1–12. If a real future reigning king is meant, it would imply that the two passages were not fully incorporated by the redaction, which introduces passages of various origin in Isaiah 13–39. On the basis of observations made elsewhere, the wording itself would not preclude a theocratic interpretation referring to the nation or the kingship of Yahweh. Isaiah 13–39 certainly contains other passages referring to Yahweh as king, such as 24:23 and probably also 33:17.

We have no hesitation about including Mic. 5:1–5 (Eng. vv. 2–6) with the Isaianic evidence.[14] Taken as a whole, Micah 4–5 is an exilic or postexilic message of salvation. The redaction of

---

11. For the preredactional situation of the texts, see above, Chapter 6, and the references there.

12. The reader should see the discussion of the individual passages in Becker, *Isaias*, pp. 49–50 (Isa. 4:2), 53–58 (7:10–16), 58–60 (8:23— 9:6 [Eng. 9:1–7]), 61–62 (11:1–5).

13. Hans Wildberger, *Jesaja*, BK 10 (Neukirchen: Erziehungsverein, 1972–), pp. 604, 620–21, 622–23. Rehm. *Der königliche Messias*, pp. 256–57, and Seybold, *Königtum*, pp. 103–6, who also do not take note of Isa. 32:1, apparently assume Isaianic authorship.

14. See Becker, "Das historische Bild," p. 137, and most recently idem, "Kollektive Deutung," p. 5.

the Book of Micah is related to that of the Book of Isaiah, as can be seen from the fact that the redactional passage Isa. 2:2–4 is repeated almost literally in Mic. 4:1–3. Its perspective is highly theocratic. In Mic. 2:12–13, Yahweh goes before his people as king without a trace of an earthly king. In 4:7, Yahweh reigns as king on Mount Zion, and there is nothing to suggest that the kingship spoken of in 4:8–9 is to be taken in an earthly sense. If "she who is in travail" in Mic. 5:2 is interpreted collectively even by exegetes who take the one born to be an individual messianic figure,[15] it is only logical that we should find the increase of the royal nation spoken of in the "birth" of the king. This actual statement is signalized in 5:2b (Eng. v. 3b), where the coming influx of Israelites is described. The royal figure, described in individualistic terms, is substantially identical with the "remnant of Jacob" in 5:6ff. (Eng. vv. 7ff.), that is, with the collective entity. The theory that the redaction was drawing on a preexilic text (perhaps 5:1, 3, 4a, 5b [Eng. 5:2, 4, 5a, 6b]) written in individualistic terms, which was reinterpreted in a collective sense by means of additions, can find some support; it is not compelling, however, because a text's unevenness can be due to utilization of various forms and motifs.

Whoever does not agree with the collective interpretation of Mic. 5:1–5 (Eng. vv. 2–6) must assign the passage to restorative monarchism. The same is true of Zech. 9:9–10; here, however, there is no lack of evidence for theocratizing reinterpretation. An earthly king would have no relevance to the context. In 9:10, following an abrupt change of speaker, it is Yahweh himself who acts; as in Mic. 5:9 (Eng. v. 10), he removes horses and chariots from Israel. In 9:8 and 9:11–17 as well, he performs the functions of the king. In the broader context (Zechariah 9–14) there is no reference to an actual earthly king to be found;[16] rather, the king-

15. See Bernard Renaud, *Structure et attaches littéraires de Michée IV–V*, CRB 2 (Paris: Gabalda, 1964), pp. 71–72; Theodor Lescow, "Das Geburtsmotiv in den messianischen Weissagungen bei Jesaja und Micha," ZAW 79 (1967): 172–207.

16. Contrary to Paul Lamarche, *Zacharie IX–XIV*, ÉtB (Paris: Lecoffre, 1961); Klaus Seybold, "Spätprophetische Hoffnungen auf die Wiederkunft des davidischen Zeitalters in Sach. 9–14," *Jud.* 29 (1973): 99–111. The

ship of Yahweh is emphasized (14:9ff., 16–17). In my opinion, Yahweh appears in Zech. 9:9–10 in the guise of the earthly king. The kingship is thus transferred not to the nation but to Yahweh. Such a reinterpretation was also undertaken by the redaction of the Book of Isaiah in Isa. 10:21. Here the throne name *'ēl gibbôr*, "mighty God," borrowed from Isa. 9:5 (Eng. v. 6), is applied to Yahweh.[17] The theocratic movement has at its disposal two ways of theocratizing the kingship: It can be inherited not only by the nation but also by Yahweh.

Collectivizing reinterpretation of individualistic texts was congenial to the mentality of late Judaism. In 1QH iii. 9–10, the royal name *pele' yō'ēs*, "wonderful counselor," taken from Isa. 9:5, is applied to God.[18] The passage is not totally clear. If the phrase is meant to designate the one who is born of the woman in labor, we are dealing once more with the basic conception of the "birth," that is, increase, of the community. The messianic interpretation is unlikely.[19] It remains doubtful whether the *gibbôr* of 1QH vi. 30 derives from the royal name *'ēl gibbôr*, "mighty God," of Isa. 9:5 (Eng. v. 6) (cf. *'ēl* in v. 29) and refers to God. In CD vii. 16–17, the author, who is discussing the interpretation of Amos 5:26 and 9:11, states straightforwardly that the king is the community. David, king, and community are equated. In 4QFlor i. 18–19, Ps. 2:1–2 is interpreted as referring to the war of the nations against the "elect of Israel"; Israel is the "anointed" of Ps. 2:2.[20] In Rev. 12:5 (cf. v. 17; differently in 19:15) too we find the identification of the king in Psalm 2 with the community.

---

statement in 12:10 refers to Yahweh; see Benedikt Otzen, *Studien über Deuterosacharia*, AThD 6 (Copenhagen: Munksgaard, 1964); Magne Saebø, *Sacharja 9–14*, WMANT 34 (Neukirchen: Neukirchener Verlag, 1969); Joachim Becker, "Sacharja 12:10–11," in *Die alttestamentlichen Lesungen*, C, 2 (1971), pp. 52–55.

17. See Becker, *Isaias*, p. 60; on 1QH iii. 9–10, see the next paragraph.
18. Sigmund Mowinckel, "Zwei Qumran-Miszellen, 1. 1QH III,9f," ZAW 73 (1961): 297–98.
19. For a more detailed discussion, see, for instance, Johann Maier, *Die Texte vom Toten Meer* (Munich: Reinhardt, 1960), 2:74–76.
20. See Otto Michel and Otto Betz, "Von Gott gezeugt, in *Judentum, Urchristentum, Kirche*, Festschrift J. Jeremias, ed. W. Eltester, BZNW 26 (Berlin: Töpelmann, 1960), pp. 3–23, esp. pp. 8–9; the authors cite a midrash on Psalm 2 on p. 7.

Contemporary exegesis of the psalms will probably find it strange that the royal psalms also bear witness to the collectivization of the idea of the king.[21] The situation can be recognized only when the collective interpretation of the psalms in general is found to be justified.[22] Before the method of form criticism, employed all too exclusively, started on its victorious course with Gunkel, the supporters of the collective interpretation included such authorities as Hitzig, Reuss, Staerk, Baethgen, the elder Smend, Kautzsch, and Wellhausen.[23] They appealed to textual observations, with repeated references to royal psalms. For us, the collective interpretation of the royal psalms is all the more convincing in that they confirm the picture of the exilic and post-exilic situation derived from other sources. Together with the evidence already discussed, they stand in the theocratic movement.

The contextual argument, supported by the textual observations, is based on the following considerations. The royal psalms in their present form are almost certainly of exilic or postexilic origin. Our use of this premise without proof may be condoned; it receives the vote of many exegetes, mostly on the basis of linguistic arguments. But in their period of origin the royal psalms cannot be explained either as texts for the royal ritual—the monarchy is no longer in existence—or as evidence of a messianic or restorative monarchism. There is no trace of messianic expectation in this era. But the royal psalms, or at least Psalms 2, 45, 72, and 110, are utterly useless as evidence for restorative monarchism because they bear the strong impress of royal ideology. The only explanation left is that preexilic ideas and forms have been given a new theocratic meaning. Only under cover of this new interpretation were ideas associated with sacral kingship pre-

---

21. For more details see Becker, "Kollektive Deutung."
22. See Becker, *Israel;* idem, *Wege,* pp. 85–98.
23. See Becker, *Wege,* pp. 85–86; idem, "Kollektive Deutung," p. 8, esp. n. 54. Specialized treatments: G. B. Gray, "The References to the 'King' in the Psalter in Their Bearing on Questions of Date and Messianic Belief," *JQR* 7 (1895): 658–86; Heinrich Weinel, "mšḥ und seine Derivate," *ZAW* 18 (1898): 1–82, esp. 69–79.

served in the Old Testament. The earthly monarchy as such is no longer relevant; it is a grandiose conception from the past, to be taken up and reinterpreted. Restorative monarchism would never have made use of forms embodying sacral kingship. It reduces the kingship to a small scale compatible with Yahwism. The same argument applies to passages like Isa. 8:23—9:6 (Eng. 9:1-7); 11:1-5; Mic. 5:1-5 (Eng. vv. 2-6); and Zech. 9:9-10. This is not the language of restorative monarchism.

Besides the contextual argument, there is a further consideration worth heeding: the relationship between the psalms of Yahweh as king,[24] the Zion hymns,[25] and the royal psalms. Each of these groups comprises a section of the repertory of ideas found in exilic and postexilic preaching of salvation; the scenery merely changes a little as the camera pans. The ideas of the kingship of Yahweh, of Zion as Yahweh's royal residence (including the motif of the nations' attack), and of the nation on Zion as the inheritor of the Davidic monarchy characterize the three respective groups, but in such a way that the boundaries are fluid. All three spheres of thoughts are present in Deutero-Isaiah, the most important witness on behalf of exilic and postexilic hope for salvation. Now, if the psalms of Yahweh as king and the Zion hymns are of exilic or postexilic origin[26] and are outspokenly theocratic, so are the royal psalms, among which Psalms 2 and 110 are most closely associated with the two other groups. Like the idea of the Davidic monarchy, the kingship of Yahweh and Zion theology are constructs based on preexilic circumstances. The complex of "Jerusalem cult tradition," elsewhere suppressed, survived in modified form in these three groups of psalms. The royal psalms

---

24. Psalms 47, 93, 96–99; also Psalms 29, 33, 100, 145, 146, 149, and others.

25. Especially Psalms 46, 48, 76.

26. Even Gunkel, who considers the royal psalms preexilic and interprets them as referring to the actual monarchy, could never be convinced to the contrary, in contrast to Mowinckel, who recognizes that the three groups belong together and erroneously but logically understands them as preexilic liturgical texts. On the Zion hymns, see Gunther Wanke, *Die Zions-theologie der Korachiten in ihrem traditionsgeschichtlichen Zusammenhang*, BZAW 97 (Berlin: Töpelmann, 1966).

were in fact composed with collective meaning, with the help of materials and formulas bearing the stamp of preexilic ideas.[27]

The individual points in the text that argue for the collective interpretation have been listed elsewhere.[28] We shall content ourselves therefore with a few references, but we wish to emphasize the value of a complete listing of the relevant passages.

There are several highly convincing instances outside the royal psalms proper. The "anointed" or "king" in Ps. 28:8-9; 1 Sam. 2:10; Hab. 3:13; Ps. 84:10 (Eng. v. 9), when the context is considered without bias, appears to refer in each case to the nation. In Ps. 80:16, 18 (Eng. vv. 15, 17), the expressions "son," "man of thy right hand," and "son of man," which probably derive from the sphere of royal ideology, obviously stand for Israel. Psalms 61:7-8 (Eng. vv. 6-7) and 63:12 (Eng. v. 11), assuming an exilic or postexilic date, are difficult but deserve mention. Earlier collective interpretation of the psalms repeatedly cited Ps. 105:15. Certainly we have here a transfer of the expression "my anointed," but it is based on the anointing of prophets, not the king.[29] More apposite is Ps. 122:5. Here the thrones of the house of David are mentioned in passing, almost as a gloss. They attest in their own fashion that the theocratic movement, without representing hopes for a concrete monarchy, is nevertheless interested in the idea of the Davidic kingship.

We shall cite the royal psalms in the order of the demonstrability of the situation in question. The subjective conviction that the interpretation is correct can sometimes be stronger. In Psalm 89, it is primarily in verse 39 (Eng. v. 38) that the evidence for the collective interpretation of the anointed appears. This is acknowledged even by exegetes who claim no preference for the

---

27. Contrary to Claus Westermann, "Zur Sammlung des Psalters," *ThViat* 8 (1961/62): 278-84, reprinted in his *Forschung am Alten Testament*, TB 24 (Munich: Kaiser, 1964), pp. 336-43, esp. 342; in view of the strange peripheral position of the royal psalms within the Psalter, Westermann concludes that there was merely a second—and messianic—reinterpretation of the texts.

28. See Becker, "Kollektive Deutung," pp. 10-20.

29. See above, Chapter 6, note 13.

collective interpretation of the psalms.[30] Psalm 144, a late antho-logical composition, is characterized by verses 12–15 as a prayer of the community. Psalm 2 is fundamentally a Zion hymn involv-ing the motif of the attack by the nations, except that the nation of Israel appears in the guise of the king. Toward the end (vv. 10–12), the theocratic perspective of the author dominates, so that the earthly king, referred to only as an ideal, vanishes totally from the picture. Psalm 18 is historicized as a prayer of David, but especially in the two final verses betrays the fact that the real speaker is neither David nor some other king, but the royal nation. The "anointed" of Ps. 132:10 stands in quasi-parallelism with the "righteous" (v. 9). This late composition refers neither to a reigning descendant of David nor to a messianic king of the future; the "anointed" is present. The point of the psalm is Yah-weh's choosing of Zion and the well-being of the nation (vv. 13ff.). It is at once a Zion hymn, a psalm of Yahweh as king (see vv. 7–8), and a royal psalm to be interpreted collectively. Psalm 110 moves in the atmosphere of a Zion hymn and psalm of Yah-weh as king, with emphasis on the motif of vengeance upon the nations. The one who acts in the battle against the nations (vv. 5–7) is Yahweh the king, not the "king" introduced at the begin-ning of the psalm, who is not to be understood literally. The state-ment "He will drink from a brook [of blood] during the cam-paign [not 'by the way']" (v. 7) is a highly poetic expression for the bloodbath to come; it lies on the same plane as verses 5–6, and has the same grammatical subject. I consider Psalm 72 to be a description of the royal nation in the guise of Solomon. Verses 8–11 may be compared with such passages as Isa. 45:14; 49:7, 22–23; 60:14. If verse 17b refers to the blessing of Abraham (see Gen. 12:3, etc.), our interpretation would be confirmed, because this blessing applies to Israel. Psalm 45 has been interpreted as an allegory of the relationship between the bride Israel and the

---

30. For example, Rudolf Kittel, *Die Psalmen*, KAT 13, 3d ed. (Leipzig: Deichert, 1914), ad loc.

messiah.[31] None of the messianological prerequisites are present, however.[32] The interpretation of the Targums, rabbinic Judaism, and above all the church, which stands in the background, is a different matter.[33] The biblical psalm pictures the relationship between the bride Israel and Yahweh. This is also the opinion of Loretz,[34] who, however, shifts this understanding to the irrelevant sphere of later secondary interpretation. The situation in Psalm 45 is thus that the kingship is transferred to Yahweh, as in Isa. 10:21 and Zech. 9:9–10, while Israel appears in the role of a bride (interpreted collectively). Earlier scholarship not infrequently interpreted the royal worshiper of Psalm 101 as the nation.[35] Finally, even in the case of Psalms 20 and 21 we might have imitative forms, formally inspired by the situation of a royal liturgy but in fact referring to the community.

---

31. See Raymond Tournay, "Les affinités du Ps. XLV avec le Cantique des Cantiques et leurs interprétation messianique," in International Organization for the Study of the Old Testament, *Congress Volume, Bonn 1962,* VT.S 9 (Leiden: Brill, 1962), pp. 168–212.

32. See Becker, *Israel,* pp. 80–90. The conclusion reached on p. 81 holds despite the statement of Rembert Sorg, *Ecumenic Psalm 87* (Fifield, Wis.: King of Martyrs Priory, 1969), p. xiv. Sorg proposes a rereading of Psalm 87 in terms of the relationship of the bride Israel to the messiah.

33. See L. Robitaille, "L'Église, épouse du Christ, dans l'interprétation patristique du Psaume 44(45)," *LTP* 26 (1970): 167–79, 279–306; 27 (1971): 41–65.

34. Oswald Loretz, *Das althebräische Liebeslied,* AOAT 14/1 (Kevelaer: Butzon, 1971), esp. pp. 67–70.

35. See, for example, Friedrich Baethgen, *Die Psalmen,* HK sec. 2, vol. 2, 2d ed. (Göttingen: Vandenhoeck, 1897), ad loc. For a survey of scholarly opinion, see Otto Kaiser, "Erwägungen zu Ps. 101," *ZAW* 74 (1962): 195–205; Kaiser himself concludes that the psalm is a preexilic liturgical document.

12

The Messianological Vacuum

The theocratic movement expresses its convictions not only positively in terms of the immediate kingship of Yahweh, the transfer of earthly power to foreign rulers, and the collectivization of the idea of the king, but also negatively in messianological silence during the exilic and postexilic period. The following writings, some of which are already outside the Old Testament, deserve mention in this regard: Joel, Obadiah, Malachi, the Book of Zephaniah, Trito-Isaiah, the Priestly source of the Pentateuch, the eschatological portions of the Psalter, the Chronicler's history, Sirach, Daniel,[1] Tobit, Judith, Esther, Baruch, Wisdom of Solomon, 1–4 Maccabees, large portions of Ethiopian Enoch (1–36, 101–8), Slavonic Enoch, and the Assumption of Moses.[2] The books of an eschatological cast in particular admit an argument from silence; in them we should expect to find the figure of a messiah if one had been present in the hopes and expectations of the age. The messiah is by no means a necessary concomitant of hopes for salvation. A distinction, however inadequate, must be made between the hopes of eschatology and those of eschatological messianism. Essential to messianism is the figure of a savior, more specifically a royal figure of Davidic lineage. Until the second century B.C. one searches in vain for such a figure.

Scholarship has been concerned to fill this incomprehensible

---

1. The son of man in Dan. 7:13–14 is a symbol of the nation of the holy ones of the Most High.

2. On the apocalyptic documents that envision a messianic figure, see below, Chapter 14.

79

vacuum.[3] The Chronicler's history plays a major role. Since it came into being between 400 and 200 B.C., it furnishes a real test case. We are confronted with a grotesque dilemma: It is either intensely messianic or totally unmessianic.

The messianic reading[4] relies primarily on the glorification of David and Solomon, as though the Chronicler were writing history from prophetic perspective to evoke the messianic kingship. It is well known that the author omits negative or purely secular aspects in the life and work of the two kings. The silence of the books of Ezra and Nehemiah, which approximately define the historical standpoint of the Chronicler, is considered eloquent by the supporters of the Chronicler's messianism. As a negative counterpart it is actually meant to arouse messianic expectations (see, for example, Neh. 9:34–37). It is stressed that 1 Chronicles 17 incorporates the Nathan prophecy of 2 Samuel 7, and 1 Chron. 17:11 is even found to accentuate the messianism implicit in 2 Sam. 7:12. The textual alteration in 1 Chron. 17:11 ("one of your own sons") is interpreted so that "your offspring" refers to the messiah himself, who will later come forth from one of the descendants of David. In addition, the theory goes, the Chronicler did not change the promise in Nathan's prophecy that the Davidic dynasty would endure forever (1 Chron. 17:12, 14) and even left out the reference to any iniquities committed by the house of David (1 Chron. 17:13). Other expressions of the endurance of the Davidic dynasty are found in 1 Chron. 28:4–7

---

3. According to Luiz Bertrando Gorgulho, "Ruth et la 'Fille de Sion,' mère du Messie," *RThom* 63 (1963): 501–14, Ruth symbolizes the daughter of Zion as mother of the messiah; Henri Cazelles, "L'enfantement de la Sagesse en Prov. VIII," in *Sacra pagina*, 1:511–15, sees in the birth of Wisdom a postexilic transcendentalizing of messianic faith. Other pertinent studies are cited by Coppens, "Relève," p. 111.

4. See Arie Noordtzij, "Les intentions du Chroniste," *RB* 49 (1940): 161–68; Adrien-Marie Brunet, "La théologie du Chroniste," in *Sacra pagina*, 1:384–97; Von Rad, *Theology*, pp. 347–54; David Noel Freedman, "The Chronicler's Purpose," *CBQ* 23 (1961): 436–42; William F. Stinespring, "Eschatology in Chronicles," *JBL* 80 (1961): 209–19; Robert G. North, "Theology of the Chronicler," *JBL* 82 (1963): 369–81; Poulssen, *König*, pp. 168ff., 171–72, 174; James D. Newsome, Jr., "Toward a New Understanding of the Chronicler and His Purpose," *JBL* 94 (1975): 201–17 (the Chronicler's history comprises only 1 and 2 Chronicles and was composed between 538 and 515 B.C. to embody the hopes occasioned by Zerubbabel).

and 2 Chron. 13:4–8 (both new) as well as 2 Chron. 21:5–7 (parallel to 2 Kings 8:17–19). Finally it is pointed out that the reference to the Exodus is suppressed in 2 Chron. 6:11 (cf. 1 Kings 8:20–21) and is replaced by a reference to the Davidic monarchy in 2 Chron. 6:40–42 (cf. 1 Kings 8:51, 53).[5]

According to other authors, who we are convinced are correct, the Chronicler's history is totally theocratic and unmessianic.[6] The glorification of David and Solomon does not illustrate any interest in the kingship as such. In what is probably anti-Samaritan polemic, the rulers are depicted as founders of the Jerusalem temple and its cult. The Chronicler shares the cultic interest of the P writer, who however makes use of the Sinai background. This anti-Samaritan polemic explains the suppression of references to the Exodus. What the Samaritans lacked was not acknowledgment of Moses, whom they even played off against Jerusalem, but acknowledgment of the legitimacy of the temple established by David and Solomon. If anything, the glorification of the two rulers is evidence *against* messianism, for such kingship would be far too sovereign and could not be harmonized with the relatively jejune and peripheral royal figure found in the Deuteronomistic writings and above all in the Book of Ezekiel, which is close to the Chronicler in spirit.

Redactio-critical comparison with the Deuteronomistic History furnishes positive evidence against messianic intentions on the part of the Chronicler. The rehabilitation of Jehoiachin, with which the Deuteronomistic History eloquently closes, is replaced by the edict of Cyrus (2 Chron. 36:22–23; Ezra 1:1–4). While the Deuteronomist focuses on the descendants of Jehoiachin, for the Chronicler the line runs from Jehoiachin through Zedekiah to

---

5. Lescow, "Geburtsmotiv," pp. 205ff., interprets 1 Chron. 22:9 as a messianic passage.

6. See Plöger, *Theocracy*; André Caquot, "Peut-on parler de messianisme dans l'oeuvre du Chroniste?" *RThPh* 99 (1966): 110–20; Baltzer, "Ende," pp. 39–40; Kellermann, *Nehemia*, esp. pp. 96–97; idem, *Messias*, pp. 111–14; Steck, "Problem," p. 453; Mosis, *Untersuchungen*, pp. 211–14, also p. 53, n. 32; pp. 161–62, n. 102. Mosis argues impressively (see above, Chapter 7, note 3) that the Chronicler does indeed harbor hopes for future salvation, but this question may be left unresolved. As far as I can see, the important studies by Welten and Willi do not deal with our question.

Cyrus.[7] Thus monarchism, even messianic monarchism, is diverted. The theocratically inclined Chronicler reveres David and Solomon as founders of the cult; for the rest, his concern is the royal sovereignty of God, who has now appointed other earthly rulers. This perspective is supported by the way the Chronicler neutralizes the politically explosive events surrounding Zerubbabel and possibly Nehemiah. Zerubbabel's only function is the restoration of a theocratic community and its temple. The prophecy of Nathan, which gives voice to monarchistic hopes in the Deuteronomistic History, loses this specificity in the Chronicler's work.[8] The textual alteration in 1 Chron. 17:11 draws attention to Solomon as builder of the temple, a propensity that is also felt in 1 Chron. 22:10 and 28:4–7. It is a gross misunderstanding to find (messianic) monarchism in 1 Chron. 17:11 in particular.[9] The unconditional nature of Nathan's prophecy as expressed in 2 Sam. 7:14–16 is even weakened in 1 Chron. 17:13–14 by omission of the reference to any iniquities. Mention of eternal endurance of the dynasty is probably due to unconsidered incorporation of the original text. The text of 2 Sam. 7:16 ("Your house and your kingdom shall be made sure for ever before me") is given a theocratic turn in 1 Chron. 17:14 ("I will confirm him in my house and in my kingdom for ever"). The Chronicler in fact views the kingship of David and Solomon as participation in the kingship of Yahweh.[10] Yahweh's kingship, however, is not tied to its earthly representatives.

---

7. See Baltzer, "Ende," pp. 39–40. Baltzer's conclusion is disputed by Mosis, *Untersuchungen,* pp. 211–14 (see above, Chapter 7, note 16). Above all, the Chronicle omits the Gedaliah episode, which has no significance for him. He emphasizes that all of Judah goes into exile.

8. The point is well made by Mosis, *Untersuchungen,* esp. pp. 89–94.

9. For example, Von Rad, *Theology,* 1:351, n. 9; Kurt Schubert, *Die jüdischen Religionsparteien in neutestamentlicher Zeit,* SBS 43 (Stuttgart: Katholisches Bibelwerk, 1970), p. 10, n. 2; Dexinger, "Entwicklung," pp. 16–17.

10. See the passages cited above in Chapter 7, note 15.

13

"Late Judaism"

In "late Judaism" (second and first centuries B.C.) there exists a genuine messianic expectation, which will be the subject of the next chapter. First, however, other tendencies of the era must be discussed, which illustrate once more the appropriateness of our concentration on the contemporary historical setting.

The Book of Sirach,[1] written around 180 B.C., as a piece of Wisdom Literature does not indulge in future hopes for salvation. They are not totally lacking, however, as the prayer in 36:1-22 and the Elijah passage (48:10-11) show. Especially in 36:1-22 the argument from silence with respect to messianic hopes is legitimate. He is full of enthusiasm for the high priest Simon II (50:1-21), who held office around 200 B.C., and drops his cloak of reserve when recalling the everlasting covenant with Aaron (45:7, 15) and with Phinehas (45:23-25; see also 50:24 [Hebrew]), which he considers to be still in force for the priesthood of his own day. In contrast, there is a dearth of passages referring to the Davidic monarchy. In 45:25, which is textually difficult, the covenant with David is mentioned only by way of comparison. It is obviously restricted;[2] the theme of the passage is the covenant with Phinehas. In 47:21-22, we do not get the impression that the author hopes the kingdom of Solomon will endure

---

1. On the messianological question: John F. Priest, "Ben Sira 45,25 in the Light of the Qumran Literature," *RdQ* 5 (1965/66): 111-18 (favorable to royal hopes); P. Zerafa, "Priestly Messianism in the Old Testament," *Ang.* 42 (1965): 315-45, esp. 335ff. (against Davidic messianism); André Caquot, "Ben Sira et le messianisme," *Sem.* 16 (1966): 43-68 (against royal hopes); Coppens, "Relève," pp. 32-33, 111-15.
2. A different reading is that of Priest, "Ben Sira."

forever; he is merely making a historical allusion. In 49:4–6 he speaks of the monarchy with a degree of resignation. Therefore it is probably wrong to find concrete hopes for a Davidic king in 47:11. This view is confirmed indirectly by the thanksgiving litany—not preserved in the Septuagint—that follows 51:12. Here the house of David and the chosen sons of Zadok stand in parallel. The passage, with its dyarchic messianism in the manner of the Dead Sea Scrolls, was presumably not written by Ben Sirach.[3]

Even more than the Zadokite priesthood, the Hasmonean dynasty was to become the object of national hopes, a situation running absolutely counter to Davidic monarchism. The First Book of the Maccabees, written in Hebrew around the year 100 B.C., reproduces the view of extensive circles when it hails Hasmonean rule, which brought national independence for the first time since the end of the monarchy, as a new salvation ordained by God. The Hasmonean ideology is given discreet but effective expression in the form of archaizing historiography.[4] The author ignores the postexilic era and gives the appearance of an uninterrupted transition from the period of the monarchy to the Hasmonean period. The reference in 1 Macc. 2:57 to the eternal kingship of David cannot be meant seriously, and should be taken as a traditional flourish. The Hasmoneans conquer Jerusalem and make war against the "aliens" as David did in the past. In 14:4–15, the author extols the time of blessing under Simon (142–135 B.C.) as though the day of salvation had come. In 14:41–47, Simon, like his predecessor Jonathan, is hailed by the people not only as their prince but also as high priest. That there was vehement opposition we learn only from the documents of the Qumran movement and from Josephus. Nevertheless, the tactfully cautious reference to a prophet to come[5] suggests the problems raised

---

3. Joseph Trinquet, "Les liens 'sadocites' de l'écrit de Damas, des manuscrits de la mer morte et le l'Ecclésiastique," *VT* 1 (1951): 287–92; Trinquet suggests that the section is an addition of Essene origin.

4. See Diego Arenhoevel, *Die Theokratie nach dem 1. und 2. Makkabäerbuch*, WSAMA.T 3 (Mainz: Grünewald, 1967), esp. pp. 40–50 and 58–69. Kellermann, *Messias*, pp. 64–68, makes the same point independently of Arenhoevel.

5. In 14:41; see also 4:46 and 9:27.

by this step, considered illegitimate by the Essenes. There is no doubt in the author's mind, however, that the prophet will legitimize the position of the Hasmoneans. In order to discredit the Zadokite high priesthood, which was exalted by the Essenes, he goes to great pains to depict its last representatives, who were pro-Hellenistic, in a negative light. Thus Alcimus is represented as a traitor in 7:12–25, without de facto authority. The Hasmoneans, as it were, took possession of an empty throne. It is insinuated repeatedly that Mattathias and his sons brought deliverance (see especially 5:62). In 2:54, Phinehas, the grandson of Aaron, is given out to be the ancestor of the Hasmoneans. The zealous action of Mattathias in 2:24–27 makes him a Phinehas *redivivus* (cf. Num. 25:6ff.). The author avoids calling the Hasmoneans by the title "king," which they bore from the time of Aristobulus I (104–103 B.C.); he calls them "princes" in the ancient fashion.

The Second Book of the Maccabees is also pro-Hasmonean; but, as Arenhoevel shows, it does not develop a real Hasmonean ideology. Its concern is the timeless theocratic sovereignty of God over his city Jerusalem; no theological importance is ascribed to his earthly regent.

Kellermann[6] has undertaken to demonstrate a pro-Hasmonean recension of the Chronicler's history. In the list of priestly divisions in 1 Chron. 24:7ff., he claims, the division of Jehoiarib has been artificially given a privileged position. But according to 1 Macc. 2:1 and 14:29, Jehoiarib is an ancestor of the Hasmoneans. In addition, the name Joiarib has been interpolated in Neh. 11:10 and 12:6, 19. Finally, the territory described in Nehemiah 11 coincides with the extent of Hasmonean sovereignty.

According to Kellermann,[7] the letter contained in 2 Macc. 1:10—2:18 also betrays a pro-Hasmonean attitude. Here Judas Maccabaeus is given equal rank with Moses (2:11), Solomon (2:12), and Nehemiah (1:18ff.; 2:13–14). Aristobulus, to whom the letter is sent, is addressed with accentuated correctness as

---

6. *Nehemia*, pp. 103–13.
7. *Ibid.*, pp. 115–24.

a Zadokite priest (1:10). The author is attempting to gloss over the Hasmoneans' lack of legitimacy.

Sahlin[8] proposes the theory that, in the son of man of Dan. 7:13-14, the Book of Daniel means to designate Judas Maccabaeus cryptically as the messiah. But it is well known that for the author of the Book of Daniel the Maccabean revolt is only "a little help" (Dan. 11:34). Equally improbable is the Maccabean interpretation of Psalms 2 and 110, still found today.[9]

The flexibility of hope for salvation, which has been demonstrated repeatedly, would lead us to expect that an ideology also grew up around Herod.[10] He rebuilt the temple, an act well suited to awakening ideas of royal deliverance on the model of Solomon and Zerubbabel and on the basis of the Nathan prophecy. It is claimed that there were attempts to prove the Davidic lineage of Herod.[11] Josephus records occasions when Herod was miraculously delivered,[12] which could serve as legends indicating that he was chosen by God. The Herodians mentioned in Mark 3:6; 12:13; and Matt. 22:16 were probably political allies of Herod Antipas and are not evidence for a lasting Herod ideology. Their identification with the Essenes, who, strangely, are not mentioned elsewhere in the New Testament, remains hypothetical. Josephus attests to Herod's respect for the Essenes; this esteem is hardly sufficient to explain the term *Herodians*.

---

8. Harald Sahlin, "Antiochus IV. Epiphanes und Judah Makkabäus," *StTh* 23 (1969): 41–68.

9. See Becker, *Wege*, pp. 100–101, esp. note 6.

10. See Abraham Schalit, *König Herodes*, SJ 4 (Berlin: De Gruyter, 1969), pp. 450–82; Kellermann, *Messias*, pp. 55–57; see, however, the critical review of Schalit's book by K. Müller in *ThRv* 67 (1971): 352–59, esp. 356–59, where "Herodian messianism" is rejected.

11. This claim is opposed by Müller in his review, pp. 358–59. It is known from Josephus *Antiquities* 14. 1. 3 that Nicholas of Damascus, Herod's court historiographer, constructed a Jewish genealogy for Antipater, Herod's father.

12. See *Antiquities* 14. 15. 11 and 13; 15. 10. 5.

14

The Threshold
of the New Testament

It is on the threshold of the New Testament that we first encounter a real messianism.[1] It is not the seamless continuation of the restorative monarchism of the exilic and early postexilic period; it is a new outgrowth of anti-Hasmonean, anti-Roman, and anti-Herodian tendencies. The messiah is aroused by God; although he will be a descendant of David, he has no fixed genealogy. This is not the same thing as royalist fidelity to the royal family in restorative monarchism. It is both new and characteristic, furthermore, that interpretation of Scripture is influential: In the sacred Scriptures the messiah is proclaimed in advance.

The messianism of "late Judaism," however, must not be judged by the measure of New Testament fulfillment.[2] It therefore does not correspond to the expectations with which we approach the sources. The messiah remains in a strictly earthly context and is not conceived of as a superhuman figure dwelling in eternity. A possible exception in this respect is the expectation of the Son of man and the messianic texts influenced by this expectation. It must also be kept in mind that expectation of a messiah does

---

1. Among the more recent studies, see Pierre Grelot, "Le Messie dans les apocryphes de l'Ancien Testament," in *La venue du Messie*, ed. É. Massaux et al., RechBib 6 (Bruges: Desclée, 1962), pp. 19–50; Schubert, "Entwicklung"; Coppens, *Messianisme royal*, pp. 33–35, 119–25; Kellermann, *Messias*, pp. 91–106, 114–23; Shmarjahu Talmon, "Typen der Messiaserwartung um die Zeitenwende," in *Probleme biblischer Theologie*, pp. 571–88; Dexinger, "Entwicklung," esp. pp. 18–31, 239ff.
2. This is emphasized by Talmon, "Messiaserwartung."

not seem to have been a general feature of Judaism. In the over-all context of hopes for deliverance and salvation, the messiah was more a peripheral figure without a real salvific function. The purpose of our presentation is merely to summarize the major movements and thus round out the historical picture. We will bypass the unique christological messianism of the New Testament altogether and consider here only a few important problems that modern scholarship has still not resolved:

1. The dyarchic messianism of the Qumran Essenes. There seems to be scholarly agreement that the messianic expectation of the Qumran documents is homogeneous and characterized by the dyarchy of Zadokite priest and Davidic prince.[3] It came as a shock to traditional messianology to discover that the priestly anointed has precedence. Elsewhere, too, the Essenes attach greater importance to the legitimacy of the Zadokite priests. The prince plays a modest role like that assigned him in the earlier priestly tradition of the Book of Ezekiel. Probably also of Essene origin are the dyarchic passages—often with Christian interpolations—in the Testaments of the Twelve Patriarchs, where Levi and Judah are singled out as the ancestors of the two messianic figures.[4] Previously scholars were at a loss where to categorize these passages and occasionally associated them with the Hasmonean priest-princes.

---

3. For citations and bibliography, see Coppens, *Messianisme royale*, pp. 34–35, 121–23, and Kellermann, *Messias*, pp. 91–95. A development of messianic ideas within the Qumran documents is found, for example, by Jean Starcky, "Les quatre étappes du messianisme à Qumran," *RB* 70 (1963): 481–505; for the contrary argument, see Reinhard Deichgräber, "Zur Messiaserwartung der Damaskusschrift," *ZAW* 78 (1966): 333–43. It is unlikely that certain passages in the Damascus Document presuppose the personal identity of priest and prince.

4. See Jürgen Becker, *Untersuchungen zur Entstehungsgeschichte der Testamente der zwölf Patriarchen*, AGSU 8 (Leiden: Brill, 1970), esp. pp. 178–82. The author does not think in terms of a close association of the Testaments with the Essene movement. The dyarchic strand is clear, but the strictly messianic coloration is the work of Christian interpolation. Becker may be judging the basic text by too strict a messianological criterion; on this basis, he denies the dyarchic messianism of the document. For further bibliography see Jürgen Becker, "Die Testamente der zwölf Patriarchen," in *Jüdische Schriften aus hellenistisch-römischer Zeit*, ed. W. G. Kümmel (Gütersloh: Mohn, 1973–), 3:26, n. 19. To the passages from the Testaments of the Twelve Patriarchs should be added Jub. 31:9–23.

2. Non-Essene messianic expectation. This refers to Davidic messianism that does not look for the priestly messiah of the Essene movement. It is impossible to say definitely to which circles of Judaism (which was highly heterogeneous before A.D. 70) these texts should be ascribed. Pharisaism is commonly suggested; the Psalms of Solomon in particular, with their ardent messianic hope, are thought to be of Pharisaic origin. Opinions to the contrary have recently been registered. According to Schubert,[5] Pharisaism is uneschatological and unmessianic, being part of the theocratic movement. Thus one must think in terms of other groups between the Essenes and the Pharisees, related to the later Zealots and representing the soul of the resistance to Roman domination. Only after the destruction of Jerusalem did messianic tendencies make themselves felt in rabbinic Judaism, which was shaped by Pharisaism. Messianism, however, never played a dominant role.[6]

In any event, purely Davidic messianism is well attested. Even the popular hopes found in the Gospels cannot be derived totally from Christian theology. They are in line with Josephus's accounts of the appearance of messianic pretenders, especially in the last three decades before the outbreak of the Jewish War.[7] A few texts are also found in Philo.[8] Especially valuable, because it can be dated with some precision, is the witness of the Psalms of Solomon (17 and 18), which must have originated around the middle of the first century B.C. on account of the references to Pompey. The Targums, the Aramaic translations of the Old Testament, uniformly paraphrase and interpret all the passages in question in a messianic sense.[9] Although they were edited in the

---

5. "Entwicklung," pp. 11ff. and 45ff., n. 40; idem, *Religionsparteien*, pp. 23–24, 25–31, 68.

6. See Schubert, "Entwicklung," pp. 36–40; idem, *Religionsparteien*, pp. 40–43; Dexinger, "Entwicklung," pp. 239–57.

7. See Dexinger, "Entwicklung," pp. 242–43.

8. See Kellermann, *Messias*, pp. 105–6; Dexinger, "Entwicklung," pp. 241–42.

9. See Martin McNamara, *The New Testament and the Palestinian Targum to the Pentateuch*, AnBib 27 (Rome: Pontifical Biblical Institute, 1966), pp. 219–20, 230–33, 238–52; Samson H. Levey, *The Messiah: An Aramaic Interpretation*, MHUC 2 (Cincinnati: Hebrew Union College,

Christian era, they contain in part pre-Christian traditions. Even the Septuagint sometimes translates messianically.[10] The dating of the passages in question should be reconsidered, since they can hardly go back to the third century B.C. Furthermore, Diaspora Judaism was certainly not a pacesetter in the messianic expectation of late Judaism.

3. Messianic expectation in apocalyptic literature. It would be reasonable to assume that at least the apocalyptic writings depicting eschatological history could not avoid mentioning the messiah. But it is precisely in God's eschatological act of salvation that the messiah has no significance. Thus traditional messianology is substantially relativized once more, even with reference to an age that for the most part is familiar with the figure of a messiah. The situation is understandable. The eschatological setting has no room for a messiah belonging to this world. Here all is concentrated on the dawn of the new eon. Even in the earliest apocalypse, the Book of Daniel, the messiah is superfluous; the same is true in portions of Ethiopic Enoch (1–36, 101–108), the Assumption of Moses, and Slavonic Enoch. When he is fitted into the sequence of eschatological events, there is no real motivation for his appearance. Early texts are Eth. En. 90:37–38 and 105:2 (an interpolation?). The other texts, namely, 4 Esd.

1974) (see the review by Roger Le Déaut in *Bib.* 56 [1975]: 421–24). For an earlier study, see August von Gall, *Basileia tou Theou*, RWB 7 (Heidelberg: Winter, 1926), pp. 397–440. Rabbinic tradition speaks of a messiah the son of Joseph or Ephraim, a precursor of the Davidic messiah, who is to fall in battle. See Von Gall, *Basileia*, pp. 387–88; Charles Cutler Torrey, "The Messiah Son of Ephraim," *JBL* 66 (1947): 253–77; Siegmund Hurwitz, *Die Gestalt des sterbenden Messias*, SJI 8 (Zurich: Rascher, 1958). The tradition is an outgrowth primarily of Zech. 12:10. The oldest piece of evidence is a fragmentary Palestinian Targum on the prophets (on Zech. 12:10). For a discussion of this little-known Targum, see Roger Le Déaut, *Introduction à la littérature targumique* (Rome: Institut Biblique Pontifical, 1966–   ), 1:128–30. The messiah son of Ephraim is most likely a late product of eschatological speculation and is not the subject of Zech. 12:10 (contrary to Torrey and others). For bibliography on Zech. 12:10, see above, Chapter 11, note 16.

10. On Gen. 3:15, see the study by Martin cited above in Chapter 5, note 7; also Kellermann, *Messias*, pp. 53ff., where Amos 4:13; Gen. 49:10; Num. 24:7, 17; Isa. 9:5 (Eng. v. 6); and Zech. 9:10 are also mentioned. Sorg, *Ecumenic Psalm 87*, thinks in terms of a messianic rereading of Psalm 87 (but see above, Chapter 11, note 33).

7:26ff.; 12:32ff.; Syr. Bar. 29–30, 35–40 (especially 40), and 53–74 (especially 72ff.) are late (around A.D. 100)[11] and are constrained by an established messianic expectation. The embarrassment caused by the figure of the messiah in the apocalyptic setting of the eschaton gave rise to the phenomenon of millenarianism or chiliasm. There is reserved for the messiah a period of earthly bliss preceding the eschaton proper.[12]

4. Expectation of the Son of man. The notion of a preexisting heavenly Son of man in late Judaism is of the greatest importance for New Testament Christology because it involves a transcendental messianism that comes close to satisfying Christian requirements. Our presentation of the historical picture of messianic expectation in the Old Testament need mention this theme only in passing, for in the Old Testament such ideas, to the extent that they were present at all, have been suppressed. The same fate befell the royal ideology, which may share a common origin with the idea of the Son of man (see Ps. 80:16, 18 [Eng. vv. 15, 17]). Preexistent Wisdom is nothing more than a personification. The myth behind Genesis 2–3, which is preserved in more original and cruder form in Ezekiel 28, has been historicized. Finally, the "son of man" introduced by name in Dan. 7:13–14 is nothing more than a symbol for the nation of the saints of the Most High and further evidence of the tendency toward collectivization.

We shall take the liberty of calling attention to a scholarly problem concerning the Son of man which is of critical importance in the realm of the Old Testament.[13] Does Dan. 7:13–14

---

11. The literary character and the dating of Orac. Syb. 3:46–50, 286–87, 652–56 are uncertain.

12. See especially 4 Esd. 7:26ff.; possibly also 4 Esd. 12:32–34; Syr. Bar. 29–30; Eth. En. 91:12–17. The millenarian schema is fully developed in Rev. 20:1–6, whence it receives its name.

13. Most recently: Ulrich B. Müller, *Messias und Menschensohn in jüdischen Apokalypsen und in der Offenbarung des Johannes,* StNT 6 (Gütersloh: Mohn, 1972); Karlheinz Müller, "Menschensohn und Messias," *BZ,* n.f. 16 (1972): 161–87; 17 (1973): 52–66; *Jesus und der Menschensohn,* Festschrift A. Vögtle, ed. R. Pesch, R. Schnackenburg, and O. Kaiser (Freiburg i. B.: Herder, 1975); Johannes Theisohn, *Der auserwählte Richter,* StUNT 12 (Göttingen: Vandenhoeck, 1975).

draw on an earlier more complete tradition, which flowed on independent of the Book of Daniel and fed into the statements of the Gospels and Ethiopic Enoch 37–71, 4 Esdras 13, and Orac. Sib. 5:414–15? In this case Dan. 7:13–14 would be an intermediate point in the developing tradition. Or is Dan. 7:13–14 the absolute starting point, on which all the later texts depend? This second view can account for the absence of any clear pre-Christian evidence other than Dan. 7:13–14. Ethiopic Enoch is of pre-Christian origin, but the very chapters in which the passages about the Son of man occur (37–71) may not have belonged to the earliest stratum. This suspicion has recently been bolstered by the absence of any Qumran fragments containing passages from chapters 37–71. The first view is supported by the analogy of the Enoch tradition, which clearly appears in a secondary and abbreviated form in Gen. 5:18–25. The author of Gen. 5:18–25 appears to have been familiar with a more extensive Enoch tradition, which did not find expression until later in the apocryphal Book of Enoch.[14] It is possible to imagine a similar situation in the case of the tradition of the Son of man, which is secondary even in Dan. 7:13–14 and in the later texts betrays the influence of Davidic messianism.

---

14. See Pierre Grelot, "La légende d'Hénoch dans les apocryphes et dans la Bible," *RevSR* 46 (1958): 5–26, 181–210.

15

Once More the Perspective of the New Testament

We have seen that the messianic prophecies cannot be considered visionary predictions of a New Testament fulfillment. In fact, there was not even such a thing as messianic expectation until the last two centuries B.C. Does this eliminate the traditional picture of messianic expectation? Such a conclusion would contradict one of the most central concerns of the New Testament, which insists with unprecedented frequency, intensity, and unanimity that Christ was proclaimed in advance in the Old Testament. Historical-critical scholarship can never set aside this assertion of the New Testament. We must therefore find an explanation that does justice to both the historical approach and the witness of the New Testament. A synthesis must be sought in which both are preserved.[1] To appeal to the light of faith for this synthesis is not a schizophrenic act of intellectual violence, for revelation and faith go hand in hand with a manifestation of their rationality. We are so convinced that the New Testament perspective is justified that we consider the material presented in this study incomplete. Messianic expectation has been treated only from the historical perspective. This, however, is not the messianic expectation of the Old Testament as such.

---

1. See Becker, *Isaias*, pp. 69–70, 75–77; Hans Urs von Balthasar, *Herrlichkeit* (Einsiedeln: Johannes, 1961–), 3/2:371–82. As an example of negative honesty without readiness to work toward a synthesis, see Georg Fohrer, "Das Alte Testament und das Thema 'Christologie,'" *EvTh* 30 (1970): 281–98.

93

The New Testament proceeds by means of an exegetical method common in late Judaism, which undertakes a concrete application to the present situation without regard for the original statement and its concomitant historical consciousness. The scriptural commentaries of the Essenes from Qumran, especially the almost completely preserved commentary on Habakkuk 1–2 (1QpHab), provide impressive examples of such interpretation. The Dead Sea Scrolls speak of the *pešer* ("interpretation") of a passage. Even before the discovery of the Dead Sea Scrolls, this mentality was sufficiently familiar from the Targums and Midrashim. For the most part, the classical messianic passages of the Old Testament are read at Qumran and especially in the Targumim in the same way that they are read in the preaching of Jesus, the early church, and the New Testament.[2] The distinctively Christian element is not the formal exegetical principle but the conviction that everything is fulfilled in Christ. It is this sense of fulfillment in the unique Christ event that gives rise to an application that is far more concrete than in late Judaism. This sense of fulfillment explains, furthermore, why the New Testament in many passages speaks unambiguously of visionary prophetic prediction. This "embarrassment" cannot be explained away. It would be worth devoting a study to how late Jewish exegesis treated prophetic prediction in the Dead Sea Scrolls, the Targums, and the Midrashim.

The christological actualization of the Old Testament in the New is so commanding that it confronts exegesis with the question of conscience whether the historical-critical method, which we too have employed, is in fact a way at all of carrying out exegesis of the Old Testament *as such.* Must the Old Testament not be read as it was (preparatorily) in the last stage of the history of the Old Testament people of God and then definitively in the early church?[3] The study of the bare facts of history retains its value as the domain of the historian and historian of religion but is decisively relativized. The interpretation of the Jewish

---

2. See above, Chapter 14, especially note 9.
3. We refer expressly to the discussion of this question in Becker, *Wege*, pp. 126–29 (see also pp. 9–10) and the bibliography cited there.

exegete who deals with the message of the Old Testament as a self-contained whole (already highly interpretative) and finally that of the Christian exegete who must read the Old Testament through the eyes of the New both have their proper place.

Since the conclusions of historical criticism are inescapable, we must concede that supernatural manifestations, to the extent that they are sought in visionary prediction, are ruled out.[4] The apologetic proof from prophecy cannot be cited in the naive way it traditionally has been. We must accept facts and refuse to embark on any dubious attempts to rescue the situation. Furthermore, a semicritical version of the traditional picture of messianic expectation is no longer of use to the apologist; it demands euphemisms that leave behind an even more profound uneasiness. It does not pay off for apologetics to offend historical thought. Because revelation is embedded in history, the unbeliever has the possibility of not seeing the hand of God. The burden that this imposes on our faith should not be underestimated. Experience shows that theological fallacies always appeal to exegetical facts.

It is by no means true, however, that manifestations of the supernatural, for which it is proper to look, are simply not present anymore. They must be sought in the right place, and it is not up to us to determine their extent and nature.[5] The history of Israel, that enigmatic nation, is well suited to cause the unprejudiced observer to pause and reflect. No one ever thought or spoke like this nation (cf. John 7:46). Messianic expectation is a matter not of isolated prophetic message but of the history of Israel.

Above all, we must remember that the messianic interpretation of the Old Testament, arbitrary as it may appear, is nevertheless based on the highest authority. The scriptural interpretation of

---

4. This statement refers to *messianic* prediction. That there was and is real prediction on the part of Old and New Testament prophets cannot be denied. It would in fact be strange if the category of prophetic prediction, which plays an important role in a sacral history, were totally without foundation.

5. In his address at the eighteenth Settimana Biblica of the Associazione Biblica Italiana (in *Il Messianismo*, pp. 15–16), Cardinal Bea suggests cautiously that the nature and extent of divine action are not always easy to define, and that there is here a task for the exegete.

the early church is not simply a question of late Jewish mentality; it is carried out with the aid of the Spirit (see especially 2 Cor. 3:12–18). It is one of the processes that make up revelation and are constitutive for the church. The Spirit dictates an inalienable form of scriptural interpretation. Jesus himself, according to Luke 24:32, 45, opened the Scriptures. Christ himself casts light on the Old Testament.

But the Old Testament itself and even the history that lies behind it possess a unique messianic luminosity. The cold facts themselves have something to yield. The antimonarchic movement, influential to the end, was an "error" from the perspective of fulfillment, but it nevertheless fulfilled a function in the *praeparatio evangelica* that opened the way to Christ. The monarchy was not itself the way to the goal; it needed the corrective of theocracy, which is likewise realized in Christ. Specific concrete forms of expectation like the Hasmonean ideology—but by no means the expectation of a priestly or prophetic figure bringing salvation!—were on the wrong track; but sacral history continued on, always in new directions. The apparent aimlessness of dead ends is true history, the kind which theologians would never have constructed. At the end of the course of development there stands, providentially, a truly intensive and widely accepted expectation of a messiah or even a "Son of man," on which the Christ event could build. And yet the fulfillment was once again an astonishing act of God, which made unbelief possible for Israel despite the tireless employment of scriptural proof by the early church.

If at the outset we found it easy to caricature the traditional picture of messianic expectations, we must now retract. To find Christ at every stop on our way through the history of Israel and the Old Testament is not only no deception but also a duty imposed on us by the inspired testimony of the New Testament, the meaning of which we must strive to understand.